1916.

£4

ged

The
PERSISTENCE
of the
PARTICULAR

The
PERSISTENCE
of the
PARTICULAR

Dennis H. Wrong

Transaction Publishers
New Brunswick (U.S.A.) and London (U.K.)

Library of Congress Catalog Number: 2004055372
ISBN: 0-7658-0272-4
Printed in the United States of America

Library of Congress Cataloging-in-Publication Data

Wrong, Dennis Hume, 1923-
    The persistence ot the particular / Dennis H. Wrong
        p. cm.
    Includes bibliographical references and index.
    ISBN 0-7658-0272-4
    1. Social sciences—Philosophy. I. Title.

H61.15.W76   2004
300'.1—dc22   2004055372

Contents

1

The Irreducible Particularities of Human Experience

"Theory" has often been popularly viewed with suspicion as consisting of general and abstract mental constructions in contrast to a hard, "concrete" realm of "fact" consisting of particular objects external to the perceiving mind. Facts are seen as the ultimate reality, the "really real." Popular opinion often tends to see all theories as dubious, as airy-fairy mental constructions only doubtfully reflecting the world of facts and prone to fanciful misconceptions. As has often been pointed out, this view implies an entire metaphysics and epistemology in which only the obdurate, saliently material world of facts is real, if inherently vulnerable to distortion and misrepresentation by the human mind. Dr. Johnson's kicking of a stone in declared refutation of Hume's epistemological subjectivism is the classic case. Such a view clearly differs from the skepticism at least implied in various postpositivist doctrines as to whether there is a world of objects external to us that we can apprehend mentally with any accuracy.

Theories are efforts of the mind to understand the world by abstracting from what is immediately present, which always has unique aspects, in order to envisage a broader realm or class of objects or events under which those present can be subsumed. Theory is an attempt to transcend the immediate present for the purpose of understanding and ultimately coping with in action a wider temporal and spatial realm. It therefore presupposes a mind capable of orientation to spatial distance and towards the past and future as well as the present, a mind capable of time-space distanciation, in Anthony Giddens's useful phrase. The sciences reverse the fact/theory valuation of the popular view in regarding theory as the goal and crowning achievement of the sciences. If "facts" are seen as "hard" even "brute" in the popular view, they are typically seen as "mere" facts—givens or "data"—in the scientist's conception, raw material for the construction of theories that is the scientist's task. The establishing of links, the building of bridges from one set of particular facts to another, is the goal of science and this inevitably involves ignoring what is unique about particular sets. The general propositions that purport to do this amount to "theory" in the broadest sense, even at the primitive inductive level of sheer taxonomy holding that the properties of one set of particular facts will be duplicated in another set that initially resembles them.

The popular view of facts emphasizes their hardness and resistance to human wishes rather than their particularity. The scientific view, though it may regard direct observation of facts as foundational for all knowledge, finds its raison d'être in the transcendence of particularity through generalization, which if indifferent to specific human wishes may serve human needs and goals by making useful prediction possible. Although holding opposed valuations of fact and theory, the popular and the traditional scientific views are in agreement on the foundational importance of a world of objective fact. For the scientist it may merely constitute raw material for the building of theories that are the proudest constructions of the human mind whereas popularly it is seen as ultimate reality itself and mental efforts to go beyond it are viewed with suspicion. Both nevertheless consider a world of preexisting nonmental facts to be the starting point of all efforts to understand reality.

Newer views in the philosophy of science challenge this consensus in arguing that there are no such things as perceived facts independent of and undetermined by theories. Since thinking involves the manipulation of concepts and all concepts are generalizations, thought itself departs from the sheer particularity of the phenomena its concepts purport to represent. These concepts take the form of linguistic symbols or signifiers, part of a language that constitutes a self-contained system whether or not it reflects any nonlinguistic reality outside of itself. The view that concepts are "nothing but" linguistic signifiers of a signified representation that is also linguistic, neither of them possessing any necessary relationship to external reality, is the centerpiece of contemporary poststructuralist and postmodernist thought. It goes well beyond most philosophers of science in questioning, in effect, all generalizations. Particular objects and events external to the human mind are either seen as ultimately unknowable or their very existence is implicitly doubted in a linguistic version of subjective idealism that surpasses that of David Hume.

The current disillusion with social science, which postmodernism manifests in its most extreme form, is a reaction to the extravagant claims made for social science in the past. The limits to which social science can reasonably aspire are now explicitly or tacitly recognized. But disillusion with social science is but a part, and a small part, of the larger disillusion with human progress that has been expressed so often and so forcefully in the twentieth century. Postmodernists who declare that only in the past few decades has belief in the inevitability of progress waned show a lamentable lack of historical perspective, ignoring the experiences of several generations immediately preceding their own. Every intellectual generation since the "lost generation" of the 1920s has rejected belief in progress as a Victorian shibboleth or as an even earlier delusion of the eighteenth-century Enlightenment and has symbolically identified its rejection with particular historical disasters: the carnage in the trenches of 1914-18, the interwar triumphs of fascism, the totalitarian outcome of the Russian Revolution, the Second World War, the invention and use of nuclear weapons, the degeneration into corruption and petty tyranny of postcolonial "Third World" revolutions, the "death of socialism," and most frequently and convincingly Auschwitz. The debunking of progress has been a regular preoccupation of intellectuals throughout the twentieth century though often enough the debunkers have offered their own novel suggestions for social salvation which have in turn lost credibility and generated new disillusionments after having won wide support for a time. Belief that application of the methods of science would point the way to the solution of social problems large and small, from ending war to reducing poverty and inequality, is a case in point.

The two great gurus of twentieth-century intellectuals were Marx and Freud, the Smith Brothers of modern thought as a wit once dubbed them. Both possessed an Enlightenment faith in the ability of science to improve fundamentally the human condition. At the same time, the doctrines they created have repeatedly been described as "secular religions": the intensity of conviction they inspired and the organizations of their followers have been likened to theological dogmas and the churches and sects upholding them. This has always been more plausible in the case of Marxism which projected a utopian end of history for all of humanity to be achieved by political action whereas psychoanalysis was primarily a form of medical therapy designed to "cure" the ailments of individual men and women. Freud forthrightly denied his own prophetic stature and his famous stated goal of psychoanalytic treatment—"where id was, there shall ego be"—was distinctly modest, promising merely to restore neurotic patients to the condition of ordinary frustration and unhappiness that he saw as the inevitable human lot. Moreover, Freud thought that the progress of modern civilization was necessarily purchased at the price of greater repression and neurosis. Yet Freud's skepticism about the possibilities of far-reaching improvements in the human condition did not deter many of his followers from inferring utopian prospects for society at large from psychoanalysis rather than merely benefits for individuals fortunate enough to undergo treatment at its hands. One writer even subtitled a book on the wider nonmedical resonances of Freud's ideas "the uses of faith after Freud." [1] Attempts to synthesize the collective salvation envisaged by Marx with the psychological regeneration of the individual promised by Freud have been numerous, the efforts of the original Frankfurt School having been the most influential in recent social science. Yet by the beginning of the present century faith in proletarian revolution as the road to utopia is preserved only by aging and declining political sects, and belief that the elimination of all forms of sexual repression will make people more loving, pacific, and less acquisitive has lost all credibility in the aftermath of the "sexual revolution" of the 1960s. In addition, the superior efficacy of the long, arduous, and expensive psychoanalytic treatment of neurosis has been widely questioned.

Marxism was the most elaborate expression of Enlightenment faith in progress, basing itself on the role of science and technology in perfecting the means of production and on its own role as "scientific socialism" in hastening the social revolution that would liberate the means of production and with them humanity from the fetters placed upon material abundance by the exploitative class societies of the past. The loss in credibility of Marxism has been obvious since the dissolution of communism in the Soviet Union and its former Eastern European satellites. Yet the events of 1989-91 were no more than the most dramatic manifestation of its decline. The failure of history to conform to Marxist predictions had been recognized by an increasing number of thinkers since early in the century: the falsification of the immiseration thesis, the reformist rather than revolutionary outlook of the working classes in the most advanced capitalist countries, the primacy of national solidarities and conflicts over those based on class, the triumph of Marxist parties in predominantly noncapitalist societies rather than where capitalism had reached its highest stage of development. Curiously, Marxism won its largest number of believers in the Western intelligentsia, if not the working classes, in the 1960s and 1970s, like a final flare-up from the embers of a dying fire. It even made inroads into academic social science at this time with Marx, though a generation older, joining Durkheim and Weber in being hailed as one of the venerated triad of founders of sociology as a discipline.

Belief in the potential of the social sciences to create a body of knowledge that might positively reshape human society duplicating the control over nature achieved by the natural sciences has hardly been a world-historical force comparable to Marxism, although both are products of the Enlightenment. Loss of belief in this potential, particularly in its current postmodernist manifestations, has certainly been influenced by the failures of Marxism, but it has also had independent roots. Faith in social science, or the "behavioral sciences" as they were often then called, was probably at its peak, at least in the United States, in the decades immediately after the Second World War. Much social research was funded by government and private foundations, new research institutes attached to major universities were created and provided new career possibilities for research entrepreneurs shuttling between campuses, foundation headquarters, and Washington bureaucracies. The imminence of intellectual break-throughs equivalent to those that had occurred in the past in physics and biology was often proclaimed; what has been more recently derided as the "waiting for Newton" syndrome was widespread. Perhaps this mood was fated to dissipate when the social problems that social scientists claimed to be able to resolve stubbornly persisted, no social scientific equivalent of splitting the atom emerged, and research funds became less available with the end of the postwar boom. In any case, critics of positivist social science began to win a hearing and soon a hundred theoretical and epistemological flowers bloomed, fragmenting the unity of the social sciences which now seemed to resemble more closely the succession of transitory intellectual fashions that had always prevailed in the arts and the humanities rather than the cumulative progress and successful applications to human needs exhibited by the natural sciences. Momentous unforeseen events of which the sudden collapse of communism was the most recent and dramatic contributed to the realization that social scientists had not succeeded in charting the future or even in immunizing us from the surprises history has always had in store for us.

Two well-known modern novelists, Iris Murdoch and Milan Kundera, have, each in a single novel, eloquently expressed the view that "theory" is fundamentally useless in illuminating, let alone overcoming, the quandaries of human life when major decisions have to be made. Both of them essentially identify theory with general statements from which practical prescriptions might be derived to aid in the resolution of the highly contingent problematic situations in which human beings inescapably find themselves. Both writers considered this insight into the irreducible particularities of individual human lives important enough to invoke it, albeit allusively, in the very titles of the novels in question, *Under the Net* and *The Unbearable Lightness of Being,* and it clearly provides the central rationale or message of the novels.

In what was the first in 1954 of the seemingly innumerable— actually just over twenty-five —novels she subsequently published, Iris Murdoch presented the following imagined dialogue from a text by her central character debating the views of another major character, Hugo, a movie magnate who renounces his exalted position to become a watchmaker. "Annandine" is the character whose phrase chosen as the title of the novel closes the part of the dialogue I have reproduced here:

> TAMARUS: But life has to be lived, and to be lived it has to be understood. This process is called civilization. What you say goes against our very nature. We are rational animals in the sense of theory-making animals.

> ANNANDINE: When you have been most warmly involved in life, when you've most felt yourself to be a man, has a theory ever helped you? Is it not then that you meet with things themselves naked? Has a theory helped you when you were in doubt about what to do? Are not these very simple moments when theories are shilly-shallying? And don't you realize this very clearly at such moments?

> TAMARUS: My answer is twofold. Firstly that I may not reflect upon theories, but I may be expressing one all the same. Secondly that there are theories abroad in the world, political ones for instance, and so we have to deal with them in our thoughts, and that at moments of decision too.

> ANNANDINE: If by expressing a theory you mean that someone else could make a theory about what you do, of course that is true and uninteresting. What I speak of is the real decision as we experience it; and here the movement away from theory and generality is the movement toward truth. All theorizing is flight. We must be ruled by the situation itself and this is unutterably particular. Indeed it is something to which we can never get close enough, however hard we may try as it were to crawl under the net.²2.

Kundera's "unbearable lightness of being" refers to the absolute uniqueness and contingency of crucial biographical events in human lives. Lives are permanently changed as a result of chance meetings with particular persons, the arbitrary choice of one route rather than another on a journey, learning through hearsay at just the right moment of residential, educational, or occupational opportunities. Kundera applies an old German saying *Einmal ist keinmal,* literally "one time is no time," or "what happens once might as well not have happened at all" as he renders it, to choices and actions taken under circumstances that will never recur. There is no bridge from the past to the present or from the present to the future: we are totally at the mercy of the particular situation we confront. It usually fades into the past and is forgotten—this is what constitutes its unbearable lightness.[3]

Murdoch and Kundera can both be described as philosophical novelists, at least in these two books. Murdoch, indeed, was an academic philosopher before abandoning philosophy as a profession for her very successful career as a novelist, if not for the modest occupation of skilled craftsman chosen by her character Hugo. Kundera explicitly presents the unbearable lightness of being as an interpretation of Nietzsche's doctrine of "eternal return" or "recurrence" in *Thus Spake Zarathustra*. Nietzsche insisted that a true affirmation of life required embracing the conviction that an individual life will repeat itself in exact detail an infinite number of times, not just exhibiting a broadly repetitive or cyclical pattern but reenacting all the joys and pains attending the original experience. Kundera's emphasis is not on the life-affirmation implicit in acceptance of eternal return, but on the "terrifying prospect" of the heavy burden of responsibility that would weigh on a person who knew that his or her decisions were bound to be repeated forever. One might argue that awareness that one's choice is irrevocable, that it is for once and for all and can never be corrected or have its consequences reversed in favor of a more promising alternative, is also terrifying and a burden that Kundera indeed characterizes as "unbearable." His primary emphasis, however, is less on the burden posed by the irreversibility of such choices than on awareness of their "lightness" under nonrecurrent conditions that make it probable they will be totally forgotten as opposed to the heaviness of a choice eternally repeated.

The positions of both writers can readily be characterized as "existentialist." Murdoch had written a book on Sartre before turning to fiction. Nietzsche, the source of Kundera's idea, is widely regarded as one of the first existentialists. The emphasis of both writers on the sheer intractability of real life problems to theory, generalization, and reason itself points to the "absurdity" of life, to the world's blind massive "facticity," to the absence of any knowable "essence" that precedes sheer existence, as well as to the freedom of individuals to take unprecedented actions that are bold plunges into the unknown, a freedom that they may nevertheless conceal from themselves by "inauthentically" conforming to a standardized preconceived pattern of action, an externally imposed "role" in the theatrical sense. Kundera does not confine his thesis of the lightness of being to events in individual biographies but extends it to historical events, including famous ones:

> If the French revolution were to recur eternally, French historians would be less proud of Robespierre. But because they deal with something that will not return, the bloody years of the Revolution have turned into mere words, theories, and discussions, have become lighter than feathers, frightening to no one. There is an infinite difference between a Robespierre who occurs only once in history and a Robespierre who eternally returns, chopping off French heads...*Einmal ist keinmal*.... History is as light as individual human life, unbearably light, light as a feather, as dust swirling into the air, as whatever will no longer exist tomorrow.[4]

Historical events involve collectivities. Whatever the contribution of particular individuals in setting them in motion, they are classified as "historical" rather than merely "biographical" because they significantly affect multitudes of individual human beings. But such collective events too are unique and irreducibly particular, the product of circumstances that will never be exactly repeated. Both the "individual" and the "group" act and are acted upon in ways and under conditions that will never recur. History is a story, a narrative sequence of nonrepeatable events. Like the events of individual lives, historical events may sink into the past without leaving any trace in anyone's memory. Kundera mentions a possible war between two African kingdoms in the fourteenth century as an example and his central character is fearful after the communist invasion of 1968 put an end to the "Prague Spring" that the same fate may befall Czech history as a result of continued Soviet dominance. Far from being forgotten, however, some historical events are more likely than the events of individual lives, or even individual lives themselves in toto, to be only too well remembered yet at the same time to be retrospectively distorted and falsified, as in the case of the French Revolution. Their "lightness" consists in the fact that their uniquely singular occurrence makes possible their fictive revision, reconstruction, and reification, enabling them to become raw material for celebratory myths and heroic legends.

There is nothing very startling in the view that both biography and history are full of uncertainties, accidents, coincidences, and unanticipated consequences that are altogether contingent. What is suggestive about the statements of Murdoch and Kundera is their linkage to "theory" and the insistence on the inadequacies of theory, its inability to help us cope with "reality" affirmed by both writers. For Kundera this awareness is painful to the point of being unbearable. For Murdoch's character Hugo, on the other hand, it provides an opportunity for creativity, for the full realization of "manhood," for the freedom of choice of which existentialists have made so much, for what contemporary sociological theorists might describe as the "autonomy of agency." Both writers see theory, consisting of generalizations, as helpless to tell us *what we most urgently and intensely want to know,* which is always particular. This admission has strong implications for social theory and the controversies both epistemological and substantive to which it continues to give rise several centuries after it was first advanced as a hopeful project, most fully in programmatic form by Thomas Hobbes (although there are other candidates for the role of pioneer visionary of social science). At issue is what we unavoidably want to know, not in some reflective, purely cognitive sense, but practically in coping with the context-bound personal and historical situations in which we are caught up in living our lives, the existential realities that inexorably press upon us and force us to take them into account.

The extreme nominalism (to use the classical philosophical term for it) expressed by Murdoch and Kundera has been less imaginatively but more systematically asserted, or at least implied, by the various brands of hermeneutics, poststructuralism, postmodernism, and epistemological relativism which have supplanted the positivist or science-building ambition that dominated social theory and social science in general just a few decades ago. The renewed interest in history by social scientists whose earlier education had not been in the academic discipline studying it is also noteworthy, especially when historical comparisons are made for the purpose of highlighting the differences among the cases compared. Sometimes these perspectives reflect disappointment in the failures of the science-building project, sometimes they suggest pleasure, at least

Schadenfreude, in the evident *hubris* of the social sciences, often they seem to express a sense of liberation from the constraints of disciplined thinking both logical and empirical, or of the refinement of aesthetic taste in the humanities, while for some they perpetuate an adversarial attitude, cynical rather than idealistic or idealizing, towards contemporary dominant ideologies and institutional legitimations. This latter attitude is clearly a response to the loss of credibility of earlier adversarial doctrines from Marxism-Leninism to other versions of socialism, countercultural utopias, "participatory democracy," and ever more comprehensive welfare states, loss of belief, in short, in a host of secular "gods that failed." It is "no accident," as Marxists used to say, that so many of the leading postmodernist thinkers are former Marxists of one or another persuasion.

These doctrines cannot be equated with the Murdoch-Kundera doubts about theory that I have cited, which refer only to human lives and the events shaping them. If these lives and events cannot be foreseen or predicted, they can at least be understood retrospectively as they are by the biographer and the historian. In contrast to some of the more extreme postmodernist thinkers, Murdoch and Kundera do not in the quoted passages apply their view to theories of nature or to the natural sciences in general. Nor do they necessarily deny that many of the routine everyday actions of human beings are themselves predictable and are made possible by the successful predictions of the actors themselves including the actions and responses of their fellow actors. Only the significant, formative events in the lives of individuals and societies requiring "moments of decision" resist prediction by any conceivable theory and carry therefore the potentiality for Murdoch's creative action and the burden of Kundera's unbearable lightness.

Ordinary everyday human actions and interactions are thoroughly predictable. Indeed, in the absence of such predictability human society would hardly be possible. As a stable, recurrent, regularly "reproduced" order, society can be said to consist of the everyday predictability for its members of one another's actions. A major legitimation of the science-building project in the social sciences used to be to insist on the predictability of human behavior in opposition to an alleged belief in "free will" that saw it as capricious and incalculable, prone to take utterly unexpected and surprising directions. It was pointed out triumphantly that people wear similar clothes, eat at specific times of the day, observe common rules of grammar in speaking, drive on the same side of the road and stop at red lights, reliably count on trains and buses running more or less on time. It was overlooked that the successful "prediction" of none of these regularities depends on systematic inquiry by a group of specialists claiming to apply methods to the study of human life in society that have proven so astoundingly successful in the natural sciences.[5]

The more recent assaults upon positivist social science have reversed the argument from predictability in contending that social scientists tacitly presuppose many rules and assumptions they share with the subjects they study. They are quite unable, it is held, to disentangle themselves from the human subject-matter of their research and theorizing. Ranging from elaborate epistemological critiques of positivism to "strong" sociology of knowledge claims that the social scientist never escapes the influence of his own cultural worldview or social position, the social scientist's claim of privileged access to a realm of "objective" social facts is denied. The social scientist is fated in the language of ethnomethodology to use as a methodological "resource" what should be a "topic" subject to investigation in its own right. He or she is inescapably tainted or biased by prior involvement with the object domain under study.

That object domain consists like everything else of particular phenomena. Nominalism, the insistence that truth resides only in the particularity of objects, is, however, a matter of degree, or of different "levels," as sociologists like to say. Iris Murdoch's Hugo is a total nominalist: "Hugo only noticed details. He never classified. It was as if his vision were sharpened to the point where even classification was impossible, for each thing was seen as absolutely unique."[6] In referring to the misrepresentation of reality inherent in words, Hugo-Murdoch even brilliantly anticipates *avant la lettre* the insistence on the unbridgeable hiatus between signs and their purported referents that later became the hallmark of linguistic deconstructionism. Doubtless this reflects Murdoch's familiarity with Oxford "ordinary language" philosophy, a major contributor reflecting the influence of Wittgenstein and Austin to the vaunted "linguistic turn" in philosophy and social thought.

Logically, such extreme nominalism cannot include cultural nominalism—more often called "cultural relativism"—or a historicism that insists on the absolute specificity of each and every historical situation. A version of the latter is the dictum that "we learn from history only that we learn nothing from history," favored by historians intent on debunking popular beliefs in the putative "lessons" of history. However, the very concepts of culture and history presuppose commonalities among the individual human beings subsumed under them. Yet why, it might be objected, should nominalism stop at the level of groups? Since individuals have identities and personalities that have been shaped by unique experiences, why is it justified to classify them under general cultural-historical conceptual labels while arguing at the same time that cultures are so unique as to be "incommensurable?" Why not go whole hog and affirm a total nominalism resembling that of Murdoch's Hugo? Even individual selves can be held to have no unity or continuity, but to consist simply of strings of isolated experiences succeeding one another in time, a position amounting to a total solipsism first advanced by Hume and upheld by some later philosophers. The extreme deconstructionism of a Derrida holding that consciousness is nothing but "a play of signifiers" amounts to a linguistic version.

Insofar as cultural nominalism, the assumption underlying what has come to be known as "identity politics" reaching beyond the ranks of professional social scientists, treats the individuality of persons as nonexistent, or as utterly insignificant, it is guilty of an extreme version of what sociologists have criticized as an "over-socialized" conception of human nature. Individuals are seen as mirrors of the culture that has shaped them, as "cultural dopes" who are mere "carriers" of their culture, or as "role-players" reading from ready-made cultural scripts. Negation of personal identity and individuality is implicit in the claim that individual identity is primarily, even exclusively, formed by groups within larger societies just as much as it was by earlier assumptions that it reflected a common culture of the larger society, usually equated in the contemporary world with the nation-state.

The nominalism of Murdoch and Kundera might be described as a nominalism of decisions, choices, or critical actions and events in the lives of humans, at least of decisions, choices, actions and events that have significant consequences for individuals and groups. Murdoch emphasizes choices in what are perceived as problematic situations permitting novel and creative responses to them. Kundera's emphasis is on minor, matter-of-fact, even "trivial" decisions that nevertheless turn out to have immensely consequential unanticipated results. Murdoch's emphasis is on the creativity inherent in human experience, Kundera's on the sheer contingent transitoriness of experience. But neither of them denies the routine predictable character of much of human life, or the commonplace generalities and regularities to which it is subject. They can hardly be seen, therefore, as advocates of a total epistemological or ontological nominalism implying a theory of the futility of any and all generalizing though Murdoch's Hugo verges on this in many of his observations. As has been often pointed out in debates over postmodernism, cultural relativism, and the so-called "strong program" in the sociology of knowledge, the claims these doctrines advance are vulnerable to the Cretan paradox that if universally true they must be self-referential casting doubt therefore on their own claims to universal truth.

Murdoch and Kundera are not, of course, social theorists or preoccupied at all with social theory as such. Existentialism, to be sure, originated as an assertion of the concrete, the contingent, and the particular against the arrogant abstractions of theory. Kierkegaard, the "first existentialist," was reacting against the all-embracing pretensions of Hegelian theory. Nietzsche questioned the universality of the claims of any and all philosophers. For contending that all statements were "interpretations," he has been hailed as an ancestor by contemporary postmodernists eager to deny the very possibility of objectivity and universality. But as novelists, Murdoch and Kundera are not engaged in these battles over theory, which postdate Murdoch's novel in any case. They succeed in articulating vividly and concretely central features of biography and history that evoke a shock of recognition independently of elaborated epistemological or ontological arguments. I have chosen to cite them because I believe they have identified precisely the circumstances of human life and history that have proved resistant to social theory and social science. This resistance has by now been openly or implicitly widely recognized and accounts for the prevailing postpositivist outlook that has produced so many brands of subjectivist epistemologies and debunking sociologies of knowledge. As I have already noted, a variety of underlying dispositions is expressed in the postmodernist outlook; in addition to the wider historical and ideological context of the late twentieth century, within social science itself disappointment over the manifest failure of the most ambitious hopes and aspirations of the science-building enterprise coexists with a spirit of jaunty polemical dismissal of the illusions allegedly upheld by surviving positivist true believers as well as of any or all theories and ideologies that continue to make universalist claims.

What do we most *urgently want to know about human life and history? What questions do we hope and sometimes expect social theory to answer?* I am not thinking primarily of the questions and problems that directly guide historians and social scientists in their scholarly investigations, of what they see themselves as trying to reveal, resolve, or explain. (Regrettably, they are often less than forthright and even confused about this starting point of disciplined inquiry, "the context of discovery" as it has been called by philosophers of science.) I am thinking rather of the noncognitive existential concerns arising out of human social life in its historical context that antedate systematic inquiry. It is, after all, the existence of such concerns that legitimates the scholarly enterprise itself as more than a mere idle or antiquarian pursuit, a time-killing leisure activity that some persons are permitted to pursue in a relatively prosperous society. The questions, hypotheses, and conjectures that historians and social scientists see as directing their inquiries are not, of course, unrelated to these contextual concerns. I have in mind here, however, the kinds of questions, hopes, fears, and expectations that both antedate and legitimate historical and social science scholarship. Murdoch and Kundera's rejection of theory is relevant to these in its focus on problems in individual life and history grounded in experience that pose more than "merely" cognitive issues for scholars to explore.

Social research actuated by positivist aspirations has some real if modest achievements to its credit, but it has hardly reduced the raw contingencies and uncontrollable outcomes to which human life is subject that are so vividly stressed by Murdoch and Kundera. Nor are the truths they assert about the human condition self-contradictory, for, as previously noted, they do not ground them in any of the sweeping subjectivist and relativist theories that have flourished in the wake of the failure of social science to live up to its formerly radiant expectations. But what of the claim made by Tamarus, Annandine's antagonist in Murdoch's dialogue, that "we are rational animals in the sense of theory-making animals?" Even if it is acknowledged that all theories occlude important, often crucial, particular aspects of experience and therefore partly falsify that experience, are they all equally useless with nothing to choose between them? Does not theory-making, as Tamarus suggests, fulfill a real human need? And does not this need also require discrimination among theories and their evaluation by standards of relative truth based on some notion—dare one say it?—of at least partial correspondence to an independently existing reality? Theories may fail in enabling us to cope with the most problematic situations we encounter in practical, decisional contexts yet still answer to cognitive and even emotional needs that are part of our nature and that are not satisfied by just any theory at all. I shall attempt to address these issues in the next chapter.

Notes

1.   Philip Rieff, *The Triumph of the Therapeutic: Uses of Faith After Freud* (New York: Harper & Row, 1966).
2.   Iris Murdoch, *Under the Net* (Harmondsworth, Middlesex, UK: Penguin Books, 1954),   80-81.
3.   Milan Kundera, *The Unbearable Lightness of Being* (New York: Harper and Row, 1985), 8.
4.   *The Unbearable Lightness of Being,* 4, 223.
5.   Dennis H. Wrong, *The Problem of Order: What Unites and Divides Society* (New York: The Free Press, 1994), chapter 3.
6.   *Under the Net,* 61

2

Theory and Knowledge:
The Sciences and Humanities

Theory by definition is concerned with generality. Philosophers of science may be disinclined to consider any and all inductive generalizations as worthy of having bestowed on them the honorific label of theory, but the distinction between generality and particularity or specificity is undoubtedly the most elementary line of division between theoretical and nontheoretical statements about the world. Generality and particularity are, however, matters of degree. "No two peas in a pod are alike" in that all objects and events in experience are unique at the very least in their time-space location. A total nominalism is therefore in principle justified. Generalizing aims to reduce or transcend uniqueness, bridging time and space by grouping together different instances on the basis of attributes they have in common. Concepts do this and the units of language are concepts. Extreme versions of postmodernist relativism, therefore, regard any and all statements as instances of "theory" or "interpretation" embodied in "discourse" and extoll their own "theory" of language as the necessary basis for understanding human mentality as such. Such a view, labeled "theorrhea" by a critic,[1] eliminates any distinction between theory in the natural sciences and in the disciplines concerned with human affairs.

One prominent version of the union of theory and fact has been what Karl Popper called the "covering law" model of scientific explanation. Empirical research discloses, presumably by accepted methods of observation, the existence of particular facts and relations between them that constitute "initial conditions" to be explained. A general law positing an established relationship between two gen-

17

eral classes of observable facts is asserted. It is then noted that the facts constituting the initially observed conditions are instances of the hypothetical classes of facts postulated by the general law and their observed relationship conforms to that stated in the law. The law is then said to have satisfactorily *explained* the observed facts, or more precisely the particular relations they exhibit, and, additionally, this testifies once again to the validity of the law. It has been debated whether this model accurately describes the process of explanation in the natural sciences and it dates back to the pre-Kuhnian era. However, it certainly describes what has been the implicit or explicit goal of much theorizing in the social sciences. One sociological theorist has argued that sociology can only be considered a fully realized science when on learning of the appearance of a new social phenomenon, the sociologist instead of rushing to the scene, pencil and paper or tape recorder in hand, turns back into his study and takes down a volume from the shelf to engage in a presumptive search for the requisite established law under which the occurrence of the new social phenomenon can be subsumed and thus explained.

However, if as argued in the previous chapter what we often want most urgently to know about human affairs is the fullness of their biographical or historical particularity, the subsumption of them under a general law will hardly satisfy us. It is their particular attributes *as such* from which the lawful statement necessarily abstracts that interest us. Nor is it convincing to regard nomothetic statements in the form of laws to be the sine qua non of the imputation of causes, the sole admissible explanations of why events have taken the course they have taken. For there are certainly causal sequences of an entirely singular nature reflecting particular conjunctures of conditions and events that will never recur in exactly the same form. To say that *if* they were to recur they would produce the same result and that this constitutes recognizing at least implicitly a "covering law" is to engage in sophistry, for the very concept of "law" implies recurrent processes that conform to the same pattern. I shall return to this question in greater detail with reference to historical explanation in a later chapter. For the present, it is sufficient to observe that what we want to know may be exactly why events have followed the singular, nonrepeatable course they have followed even if we recognize that our knowledge will inevitably be retrospective and of no use in predicting future events.

Our curiosity and interest may often suffice to account for our seeking to explain nonrecurrent sequences. "Interruption, incoherence, surprise are the ordinary conditions of our life." Valéry went on to remark that their absence induces "boredom," which "we no longer know how to make...bear fruit." [2] But while we often welcome surprise and variety, we also may feel anxiety over striking contingencies and irregularities that crop up in our experience. The search for retrospective explanations of them may amount to a quest for reassurance that these disturbing unexpected occurrences are nevertheless the effects of discernible causes, thus alleviating the disquiet aroused by their novelty and unpredictability. This applies also certainly to the quest for general laws that, though rarely operating, may still eliminate the irreducible particularity of apparently irregular occurrences in showing their conformity to the overall lawfulness of the universe.

If the crucial difference between the natural sciences and the study of human affairs lies in what we want to know about these different realms of phenomena, in the case of the natural sciences we are for the most part—I shall note necessary qualifications below—simply not interested in the particular, unique properties of the objects and events they study. We do not care, apart sometimes from its time-space location, what makes this atom, chemical compound, or cell different from all other atoms, compounds, and cells. We are interested in it solely as an example of the general class of objects to which it belongs. This limit to our interest is grounded in our prescientific existential relation to material objects and natural processes. Our usual concern is with the general properties of the objects and processes that will be of service to us as means in routinely controlling our physical environment and realizing our practical ends. At times, to be sure, we may cherish particular material objects such as locks of hair, faded flowers, man-made articles of clothing as icons symbolizing particular persons and situations of which they remind us; we even create physical artifacts to serve precisely this purpose as in wedding rings, lockets, and the like. Works of art in material form are also cases in point; obviously their humanly created individuality is what makes them works of art. An excessively strong attachment to a material object symbolizing a significant person or event in the life of an individual may, however, be decried as pathological "fetishism." The term is taken from the role of objects in primitive magical and religious systems and at least suggests Freud's view of religion as the "universal obsessional neurosis of mankind." We also develop sentimental attachments to particular rocks and rills and wooded hills that are part of our natural environment.

The natural sciences, however, also include the study of nonrecurrent "historical" sequences in paleontology, evolutionary biology, and astrophysics and also may concern themselves with particular unique objects like the planets. Critics of extending the "natural science model" to the social sciences have often cherished too simple and partly antiquated a conception of the process of scientific reasoning in the natural sciences, as Clifford Geertz has cogently argued.[3] Moreover, recent post-Kuhnian "constructivist" studies of the sciences have shown that they too are partly shaped by at least the reigning social beliefs, norms, and values of the community of scientists to which the researcher belongs if not necessarily by the ideologies and belief-systems dominant in the larger society of which the scientists are members. Undoubtedly, these considerations blur too sharp a distinction between the natural and social sciences, showing both to be human "social constructions" influenced by the established assumptions of their practitioners.

Consider the enormous bodies of knowledge about real and imagined human life and experience that exist in all societies, ranging from the shared understandings of their socialized members to what is articulated and known only to classes of specialists. Despite our interest in particular nonhuman phenomena, and, more rarely, in the causation of their particularity as most evidently in the case of natural disasters, there is no real equivalent referring to the world of nature to these huge accumulations of recorded lore and information about the doings of human beings. In the advanced societies, we group together and transmit the more reliable segments of this knowledge under the educational rubric of "the humanities." There is nothing dealing with nature corresponding to literature, history, philosophy, and other fields studying the collective human experience, biographies of significant individuals, and what humans have created through the ages. Representations of particular natural objects and settings are common enough, but they usually are no more than that rather than efforts describe in the fullest detail and to account for—that is, explain—the particularity itself.

It used to be asserted by enthusiastic proponents of the "new" social sciences that the humanities consisted simply of a huge collection of past and present subjective impressions, or in the case of recorded history more or less reliable descriptions of particular time and space-bound facts. The social sciences, it was held, aimed at generalized *explanations* undercutting these heterogeneous masses of data by revealing their conformity as special cases of universal lawful sequences, just as Newtonian physics accounted for such diverse phenomena as the motions of the planets, the velocity of falling bodies, and the flight through the ether of projectiles. I think my earliest doubts about the natural science model for the study of human affairs were stirred by the realization that if I really wanted to know something about some particular social event or process, I would turn—as I still do—first to the historians, or even to trustworthy journalists. I would not then follow up this initial effort at understanding by seeking out relevant generalizations advanced by social scientists that might define or redefine the phenomenon as no more than a new case falling under a confirmed generalization. The accounts of historians, sometimes even of conscientious nonacademic reporters, often were entirely adequate to satisfy my curiosity by explaining the phenomenon in question: no sharp line could be drawn in their formulations between what constituted description on the one hand and explanation or the imputation of causes on the other.

My earliest self-consciously intellectual interests were in literature and politics, which doubtless partly induced my uneasiness when I first encountered as an undergraduate the large claims made for the social sciences. The fact that I was descended from several generations of academic historians also probably had something to do with it. My academic relatives were unimpressed by the pretensions of psychology, sociology, and anthropology perceived as new, or at least "new-fangled," social sciences. During my graduate school years in New York City just after the Second World War, I fell in with a group of literary bohemians convinced that "Dostoievski had said it all before and better." Most often they mocked the bad writing and "jargon" of sociologists, asserting, often accurately enough, that it merely stated in pretentious pseudo-scientific language what was "common sense" that "everyone already knew;" truly novel insights into the human condition required rare "literary sensibility," inherently superior to abstract reason and pettifogging fact-grubbing empiricism. Sometimes, inconsistently, fears were expressed by the same people that a fully realized social science would serve as a fearsomely efficient instrument of totalitarian rule. Huxley's *Brave New World* was the prototype for the latter claim, very fashionable at the time, though it was usually overlooked that Orwell's *Nineteen Eighty-Four*, then and now commonly grouped with Huxley's dystopian vision, assumed little progress in science apart from the invention of two-way television screens permitting surveillance of every home by the minions of Big Brother. My exposure to these aspects of the zeitgeist undoubtedly made me particularly sensitive to criticisms of what I was taught in graduate school about the unity of the natural and social sciences.

I remember once protesting to a fellow-sociologist that sociology didn't directly address what were to me the most urgent of questions, such as "Why and how did Hitler come to power?" The urgency of that particular question defined one of the chief public concerns of my generation, especially for someone who like myself had in his early teens lived and gone to school in Europe on the eve of the war. My interlocutor replied with a sweep of his hand, "We sociologists are interested in why and how *all* dictators come to power." I brooded over this afterwards and came to the conclusion that it was actually much harder to identify and explain the very specific historical circumstances that amounted to necessary and sufficient conditions for Hitler's (or any dictator's) ascension to power than to formulate a set of credible and verifiable statements about the presumptive necessary conditions for any and all dictators winning power. Examples of the latter would be: widespread social discontent, potentially violent group conflicts, the aftermath of demeaning defeat in war, charismatic power-seeking individuals, and the like. It is not hard to come up with a set of such conditions out of a broadly comprehensive and comparative knowledge of human history, some applicable virtually to all cases, others only to some of them. It is much harder to identify the precise passage from the necessary conditions, both general and historically specific, to the sufficient conditions that actually brought about the historical consequence in which one is interested. In the case of Hitler, the sufficient conditions, among others, included the increasing senility of the octogenarian President Hindenburg, the rivalry between the two conservative preceding chancellors, Papen and Schleicher, the general perception based on the most recent election that Hitler's movement had lost much popular support, the split in recent elections between the Social Democrats and the Communists.[5] The persisting mass unemployment was doubtless a necessary condition, but it was not peculiar to Germany at the time. The operative sufficient conditions, of course, also exemplify general laws or recurrences: that people in their eighties often suffer from failing mental powers, that leaders and parties of both right and left are usually divided and fragmented under crisis conditions, that new political movements wax and wane in short periods of time. These are all familiar commonplaces of experience in no way dependent on systematic social theory. If they are hardly surprising or puzzling, their conjunction in a specific location in space and moment in time, how they interact and combine, is what defines historical uniqueness or particularity. And that conjunction and the interaction that results, while certainly not arbitrary or uncaused, are not themselves subject to lawful generalization other than in Nietzsche's fantasy of "eternal recurrence."

Biographical and historical knowledge illuminates the conjunctions and interactions that produce the effects that interest us, but for the most part it has no predictive value whatever. It is our relation to this knowledge, the fact that it is *self-knowledge*, whether of particular individuals, particular societies, or of the narrative sequences of human history, that differentiates it from the subjects of the natural science where our interest in their particularity is, while not nonexistent, distinctly limited. This accounts for the voluminous compendium of knowledge of particulars—the past, the lives of significant individuals, the cultures and languages of societies other than our own, human creations in the arts—taught in the humanities and the absence of any counterpart to it in the natural sciences.

The notion of *social* theory presupposes a difference at the very least in the subject matter of theories. The antipositivist conceptions that have by and large prevailed in philosophies of social science since at least the 1960s (although, of course, they were rooted in much earlier intellectual traditions) are based on assumptions that are essentially substantive about how human nature and action differ from the object domains studied by the natural sciences. Particular researches in the social sciences may presuppose them, but they are not axioms of a truly *a priori* nature equivalent to the Kantian transcendental categories of time, space, and cause. They are based rather on beliefs about the unique generic attributes of human beings, conceptions of what Aristotle called the *differentia specifica* of man, that are substantive and even empirical if not subject to any particular time and space-bound observational or experimental test of either their verifiability or falsifiability. Such conceptions of what is universally and distinctively human are often labeled "philosophical anthropology." When they are said to be presuppositional or "meta-theoretical" assumptions, it is not always clearly understood that they are statements of a substantive rather than a purely axiomatic or methodological nature that are subject to assessment in light of the totality of known human experience. They may indeed play a presuppositional or metatheoretical role in relation to specific inquiries, but such a role is relative to such inquiries, to the particular questions asked and the kind of answers to them sought. At a higher level of generality, assumptions about the nature of human beings and the societies they create are not nonempirical for their credibility is dependent on the accumulated evidence of human experience and history even though no conceivable observational test could be adequate to confirm or disconfirm them since any such test would inevitably be time and space-bound.

Talcott Parsons famously argued that "the structure of social action" consisted of ends, means, external conditions perceived as unmodifiable, and norms limiting the selection of means.[4] He considered these four properties of action to be the equivalents in the study of human social action to mass, volume, and velocity in the study of the motion of physical bodies. The view that action could only be understood if the ends, means, conditions, and norms or selective standards apprehended in the mind of the actor were taken into account was in opposition to the rejection by behaviorism, widely accepted at the time Parsons wrote, of the explanatory status of any unobservable subjective, that is, mental or psychic, correlates of action. John Dewey's insistence at roughly the same time on the centrality of "ends-in-view" in motivating human conduct was similarly directed against behaviorism.[6]

Such a conception of human action as purposive or goal-directed, that is, oriented to an imagined but nonexistent future state of affairs rather than merely reactive to the stimulus of an existing external condition, clearly served as a presupposition for many or most nonbehaviorist efforts to explain action independently of any knowledge of or commitment to the various formulations of Wilhelm Dilthey, Heinz Rickert, Max Weber, Parsons, Dewey, Alfred Schutz, Robert MacIver, and other writers adopting a similar position in what would today be called a postpositivist or "interpretive" philosophy of social science. Parsons himself hardly intended to propose, as a student of his once misleadingly prescribed, that research into particular instances of human action should at the outset identify explicitly the actual ends, means, conditions, and norms of the actors. He was not providing a guide or directive for research practice. He meant rather that, in the absence of a dogmatic methodological commitment to a restrictive behaviorism or biologism, all efforts to understand human actions necessarily involved thinking of them in terms of his ends-means schema applied to "unit acts" linked in systems or complexes. In this sense his schema was "presuppositional" for *any* specific research into human social action. Parsons's conception was primarily directed against the Utilitarian assumption of what he called "the randomness of ends." He argued that both ends and norms restricting the choice of means to realize them were socially learned and reflected, indeed constituted, the normative order of society.

The brunt of the criticism to which Parsons was later subjected was to doubt the necessary consensual basis of ends and norms he postulated that resulted in his tendency to equate social action *per se* with conformity to norms held in common by a group. He was also charged with overemphasizing the conscious purposiveness of human action. Both criticisms were based on a sense that the world of human experience does not entirely fit the Parsonsian categories. Such categories therefore imply at the very least a general substantive conception of empirical reality even if their extreme generality precludes any particular observational test. The high level of generality of questions about the universal and distinctive properties of human action has meant that they have been considered at length by professional philosophers as well as by social scientists. They are nevertheless central to any social theory worthy of the name and clearly support frequent claims that social theorists need to possess some philosophical sophistication in addition to broad familiarity with the content of the social science disciplines. The so-called classical sociological theorists largely antedated the full differentiation of the particular social science disciplines from philosophy in the late nineteenth century, so it is hardly surprising that most of them were originally educated in philosophy. The major exception was Max Weber whose formal education was in law and economic history and who possessed a truly encyclopaedic knowledge of universal history; even at his most abstract and definitional, as in the opening chapters of *Economy and Society*, his concepts were distilled from the immense array of historical examples that makes up the bulk of that multi-volume work. In recent years a larger number of theorists have come directly out of the established social sciences, but the most prominent ones have clearly also been shaped by philosophical traditions—Parsons by Whitehead, Blumer by Mead, Goffman also by Whitehead, Habermas by the Hegelian neo-Marxism of the Frankfurt School, Berger and Luckmann as well as Garfinkel by phenomenology, Giddens by British analytic philosophy, Bourdieu by French structuralism, Coleman by the longstanding Utilitarian assumptions of classical and neoclassical economics.

Since the divisions between disciplines in the university are to a considerable extent the result of contingent events that brought them into existence at a particular time, it is unnecessary to draw a hard and fast line between philosophers and nonphilosophers engaged in social theory. The flourishing of sociology as an empirical discipline in the early postwar decades, however, led to a programmatic emphasis on the necessary unity of theory and research. Even an "incurable theorist" (his own self-description) like Parsons continually paid obeisance to "empirical research," contending that the ultimate value of his own "systematic theory" could only be confirmed by its success in guiding and finding support from ongoing research. Parsons's critics often responded to this by doubting that his abstract categories of social action and social systems advanced any empirical propositions or even contributed new insights; they amounted, it was argued, to no more than a particular conceptual vocabulary or jargon in which statements about the social world, including the findings of social research, might be formulated. In the judgment of C. Wright Mills, the harshest of Parsons's early critics, Parsons's "Grand Theory" amounted to little more than abstract verbiage restating the assumptions and conclusions of ordinary sociology uninformed by the Parsonsian dispensation.[7] Although Mills was not a positivist committed to sociology as a science-building project, he too thought that the value of Parsons's work and therefore of social theory in general should be assessed according to its yield in significantly illuminating the empirical historical world in conformity to what he called "the principle of historical specificity,"[8] misattributing the phrase to Marx rather than to its actual author, the neo-Marxist philosopher Karl Korsch.

Both Mills and Barrington Moore, Jr.[9] argued that Parsons's nomothetic quest for ever wider generalizations led him to vacuous heights of abstraction that were of little use in understanding the concrete realities of history. Rather than advocating in positivist fashion greater unity of theory and research as a corrective, both of them adopted a fundamentally historicist position, insisting that "the variety of history...is what social science is about" (Mills) and that social science must be concerned with "what history places on the agenda for us" (Moore).[10] Yet neither of them upheld a complete historical relativism or nominalism. Mills's lapidary phrase "the sociological imagination" prescribed a comparative perspective on any and all human phenomena, the location of their undeniable historical specificity in a gallery of similar but not identical types or along a continuum of variation. A total nominalism implying an interest in historical particulars strictly for their own sake amounts to sheer anti-quarianism. While recognizing the appeal of a strictly nominalist historicism that renounced prediction as a goal in resolutely denying any possible confusion of historical study with "prophecy," Moore in the end rejected such a position, opting for the comparative historical approach that his own later scholarship richly exemplified as he became perhaps the most influential pioneer of such research that has been a major tendency in academic sociology since the 1960s.[11]

Mills and Moore rejected both "Grand Theory" and "Abstracted Empiricism"—Mills's pejorative labels—the latter referring to social research conforming to the dominant emphasis in the 1950s on quantitative opinion and attitude surveys. Their position, however, was not based on any systematic epistemology or philosophy of social science but rather on their conviction of the excessive abstractness of Parsonsian theory, on the one hand, and the triviality of most current research often pervaded by what Moore's Harvard colleague Pitirim Sorokin derided as "methodolatry," on the other. Their criticism was less inspired by the hiatus between theory and research falling short of the prescribed standards of genuine science than by the failure of both theory and most research to contribute to the understanding of concrete historical situations including the momentous moral and political dilemmas posed by the crisis of the moment, that is, the Western world in the middle of the twentieth century. Both of them charged social science with, in Auden's fitting phrase, "lecturing on navigation while the ship is going down." This was especially true of Mills whose political radicalism made him an ideological founding father of the New Left student movements that emerged in the late 1950s and the 1960s. Moore was an original member of the Russian Research Center at Harvard that was a creation of the period of the early Cold War; some years later he was influenced by his friend and former associate in the OSS, the wartime predecessor of the CIA, Herbert Marcuse, who was the most influential ideological mentor of the New Left.

The views of social science of both men undoubtedly reflected their political outlooks, but they were by no means reducible to them. Mills's *The Power Elite* was clearly in part a political statement; he later wrote two straightforwardly political, even agitational, pamphlets, and his adversarial view of American society unmistakably influenced the most famous manifesto of the student New Left, the Port Huron Statement. Yet he made a point of including such conservative thinkers as Herbert Spencer, Vilfredo Pareto, Gaetano Mosca, Walter Lippmann, and Joseph Schumpeter in his roster of exemplars of the sociological imagination. Although Moore's most influential book had affinities with Marxism in its emphasis on the contribution of class conflicts and their outcomes to the making of the modern world, his later work was critical of the aspirations of revolutionary radicalism [12] and, unlike Mills and Marcuse, he remained preeminently a scholar who could never have been described as a political "activist."

I choose to mention Mills and Moore here because they profoundly shaped my own views on the goals of social science and the limits of general theory and I remain in essential agreement with what I take to be the essence of their position. At the same time, they were like all of us products of their time and place. Their reaction against the vacuity and triviality of much social science in the 1950s and the political complacency of the Eisenhower era led them into certain overemphases. One of Moore's prime examples of triviality and irrelevant quantification in social research has itself fallen victim to the relativism implied by his insistence on the necessary shaping of social science by history's agenda. He cited as a typical example of the application of quantitative expertise to an insignificant topic a statistical study, published in the major American sociological journal, of the frequency of episodes of "sexual aggression" reported by female college students.[13] A few years later, Nathan Glazer questioned Moore's imputation of insignificance on the grounds that the aggressive acts recorded, far from seeming trivial and inconsequential, would have been "a subject of considerable importance to girls, boys, their parents, deans and others." [14] One need not credit Glazer with unusual prescience to reflect that today in the wake of the reborn feminist movement of the 1970s the issue of "sexual harassment," especially on college campuses, has become a major theme of political and social criticism.

In their response to the aridity of Parsonsian abstraction and the pursuit of generality for its own sake, Mills and Moore went too far in ignoring or minimizing the existence of theoretical questions of a truly general and even universal nature which have inspired much social theory in the past. Parsons and his disciples, to be sure, often appeared to have neglected meaningful substantive answers to such questions in favor of elaborating a ponderous vocabulary in which to couch possible answers. But thinkers and ordinary people often genuinely seek answers to general questions about the nature of man and society even when they fully recognize that the answers are not likely to provide much help in resolving the existential quandaries of everyday life or the critical collective choices presented by specific historical situations. Such a quest may be rooted in a real need to be assured that the world possesses a temporally stable, determinate structure even when it is recognized that its concrete details—the trees rather than the forest in a familiar metaphor—remain irrreducibly contingent and particular. The quest can express a need for "Nomos" or for "ontological security" as in the respective language of at least two quite different contemporary social theorists.[15] Much of social theory can be seen as an effort to satisfy such a need rather than as an attempt to provide hypotheses for particular researchers or to address the historically specific problems of a given time and place. Iris Murdoch's Tamarus in the fictional dialogue cited in my opening chapter thus had a point in claiming that humans are "theory-making animals. The questions such theory strives to answer are real questions of a substantive nature, empirical questions though of surpassing breadth and scope. Answers to them need not amount to an abstract multisyllabic special vocabulary for describing familiar social and historical events and situations. Such questions are what I have in mind in entitling the next chapter "the eternal questions of social theory," although I do not presume to claim that there may not be others that I have neglected. The following chapter, "The Symbolic Animal," addresses the primary question of the *differentia specifica* of humanity as such, the subject of what has been traditionally called philosophical anthropology, and the answers to which, or the assumptions about, are presuppositional for the other eternal questions as well as for any and all social science.

Notes

1. J.C. Merquior, *From Prague to Paris: A Critique of Structuralist and Post Structuralist Thought* (London: Verso, 1986), 247.
2. Quoted by Zygmunt Bauman, *Liquid Modernity* (Cambridge: Polity Press, 2000), 1.
3. Clifford Geertz, *Available Light: Anthropological Reflections on Philosophical Topics* (Princeton, NJ: Princeton University Press, 2000), 143-159.
4. *The Structure of Social Action* (New York: McGraw-Hill, 1937).
5. I have relied for the references to Hitler's coming to power on Henry Ashby Turner, Jr.'s immensely detailed *Hitler's Thirty Days to Power— January 1833* (Reading, MA: Addison-Wesley Publishing Company. Inc., 1996).
6. John Dewey, *Human Nature and Conduct* (New York: The Modern Library, [1922] 1930), 223-237.
7. C. Wright Mills, *The Sociological Imagination* (New York: Oxford University Press, 1959), 47-49.
8. *The Sociological Imagination,* 149.
9. Barrington Moore, Jr. *Political Power and Social Theory* (Cambridge, MA: Harvard University Press, 1958), 101-102, 111-159.
10. Mills, *The Sociological Imagination,* 132; Moore, *Political Power and Social Theory*, 113.
11. Barrington Moore, Jr., *Social Origins of Dictatorship and Democracy: Lord and Peasant in the Making of the Modern World* (Boston: The Beacon Press, 1966).
12. Barrington Moore, Jr., *Reflections On the Causes of Human Misery and Upon Certain Proposals to Eliminate Them* (Boston: The Beacon Press, 1970, 1972).
13. *Political Power and Social Theory*, 129-130.
14. Nathan Glazer, "The Ideological Uses of Sociology," in Paul F. Lazarsfeld, William H. Sewell, and Harold L. Wilensky, editors, *The Uses of Sociology* (New York: Basic Books, 1967), 70.
15. Peter L. Berger, *The Sacred Canopy: Elements of a Sociological Theory of Religion* (Garden City, N.Y.: Doubleday and Company, Anchor Books, [1967] 1969, pp. 19-28 Anthony Giddens, *Modernity and Self-Identity: Self and Society in the Late Modern* Age (Cambridge, U.K.: The Polity Press, 1991), 35-69.

3

The Eternal Questions of Social Theory

The eternal questions of social theory are analogous to the eternal questions of philosophy in that they continue to be asked by successive generations of thinkers without ever being definitively answered or even with any real expectation that they will ever be definitively answered. Successive generations ask them from new perspectives often giving birth to new conceptual languages, but no cumulative progress improving upon the answers of previous generations can unambiguously be said to have occurred. In this respect social theory resembles philosophy rather than the natural sciences. Such a conception is clearly opposed to the injunction that the main task of social theory should be to provide hypotheses to be tested empirically by ongoing social research whose findings will then help determine whether the theory is to be accepted or rejected, repeated research findings confirming the hypotheses and resulting in a scientifically validated theory. The desired "union of theory and research," like the much-sought-after union of theory and practice in political action aspired to by Marxism, is unattainable in social theory. Also, when asserted as a primary goal it misconceives the purpose of much, if not most, social theory. Social theory is therefore more than the handmaiden of empirical research limited in its scope to whatever research methods may be currently available. Like the empirical investigation of particulars *qua* particulars as well as the undeniable technological progress undergone by research methods, social theory has its own autonomy independently both of the findings of empirical research and the research techniques deployed in research. Nor does this necessarily deny that there may have been some cumulation in the understanding of areas of human experience, even at a wide-ranging "macro-historical" level.

A well-established scientific discipline comes close to realizing a unity of theory, method, and empirical research, all three nestled according to post-Kuhnian philosophy of science within an accepted "paradigm." Sociology is certainly not such a discipline. Theory and research methods are subjects that students are almost universally required to study in graduate programs in sociology. Yet there is little obvious connection between acquiring some understanding of the ideas of the current " Holy Trinity" or "canonical orthodoxy" of Marx, Durkheim, and Weber on which the content of most required theory courses centers, and learning how to construct a questionnaire or to calculate regression coefficients. Theory, methods, and substantive research usually develop quite independently of one another. If as critics charged Parsons's Grand Theory had little effect on empirical research and violated Karl Korsch's "principle of historical specificity," it is also the case that methods of research, especially statistical techniques, have been frequently elaborated for their own sake. Indeed, in the 1950s C. Wright Mills complained that sociology was tending to become "the methodological specialty" lacking any special subject matter of its own. Much if not most social research is guided by the practical needs and interests of funding agencies and public policymakers independently of both theoretical or methodological considerations, or, for that matter, of the goal of preserving knowledge of certain particulars "for the historical record."

The ambition of positivist science-builders to unite theory, method, and research in scientific practice establishes a dividing line between "pure" and "applied" research. Such a project ignores cognitive needs that motivate theory at its own level whether or not theoretical generalizations encompass any particular body of data under consideration. Robert K. Merton, the most sophisticated and influential advocate of the unity of theory and empirical research, argued that much past social theory provided no more than "general orientations" to the social world and failed to suggest empirical propositions that lent themselves to "testing" by established research procedures.[2] At roughly the same time Herbert Blumer, a severe critic of sociological science-building most of whose criticism could accurately be described as anti-theoretical as well as anti-positivist, insisted that general concepts in sociology were and never could be more than "sensitizing" instruments falling far short of satisfying what we wished to know about the particular empirical cases under examination.[3] Merton's aim was to promote the science-building project while Blumer's was to debunk it, or at least to suggest its limits in satisfying human curiosity, but both of them recognized that general perspectives of an intellectually sensitizing nature dominated most of what passed for social theory. Yet neither of them fully acknowledged that an urgent human need might be served by the creation of such perspectives whether or not they contributed to the production of empirical research conforming to the canons of scientific logic and method. It is, after all, a central, even a defining feature of human action and experience that new situations are always approached with broad expectations based on past experience. The grouping of their novel distinguishing characteristics into a new unique constellation of general categories is the essence of creative thinking amounting to a synthesis that discerns the general in the particular without suppressing its particularity.

What are the major "general orientations" or "sensitizing concepts" with which human beings, and not merely academic social scientists, approach the situations they encounter, and that give rise to "eternal questions" that constitute the fundaments of the intellectual discipline of reflective and systematic social theory? The generality of the questions necessitates that they be broken down into several subordinate, equally general questions. While my list is surely far from exhaustive, I think the initial broad questions can be grouped under four broad headings:

1. What are human beings universally like? What, in short, is "the nature of human nature"? Is there, indeed, such a thing as a common human nature? The question goes back at least to Aristotle's reflections on the *differentia specifica* of human beings, on what distinguishes humanity's essence from that of other animals, although the broad question does not necessarily deny that humans and animals may also have features in common in addition to simply being living creatures. The enormous variability of human behavior gives

rise to a search for some common measure possibly underlying it. The question's scope necessitates breaking it down into several subordinate questions. The comprehensiveness of the notion of human nature requires that the concept be initially divided into separate consideration of the distinctive cognitive capacities of human beings, on the one hand, and the universal constancies of human emotions and motivations, on the other. In popular usage, human nature is usually identified with the latter, particularly with what are perceived as moral flaws, especially its more egocentric and self-interested aspects, for example, "It's just human nature to want to have one's cake and eat it too."

The emotions and basic motivational impulses of human beings, independently of their varied objects, are unmistakably continuous with those of the other animals, especially the higher mammals. This is not true of human cognitive capacities, or at least is less true to the extent of amounting to a virtual difference in kind rather than even an immense difference in degree, as has long been recognized by the singling out mind, reason, thought, consciousness, intelligence, wisdom, and other more or less synonymous mental attributes as peculiarly and therefore distinctively human. I summarize a number of these attributes in the next chapter and suggest, following George Herbert Mead, that it is the human capacity for what he called "symbolic communication" that is not just another name for them but rather the foundation of all of them. Symbolic communication or language therefore constitutes the fundamental *differentia specifica* of humankind. Language was, of course, identified as distinctively human long before Mead, but he succeeded in isolating the fundamental behavioral mechanisms underlying it. He called his theory "social behaviorism;" it was Blumer who renamed it "symbolic interactionism."

A second derivative question poses the eternal debate over the respective roles of "nature" and "nurture." One extreme answer is that just about everything—capacities, motivations, behavior—follows from the biological endowments that define the species, cultural and historical variability amounting at most to different manifestations of invariant traits rooted in the genetic and constitutional heritage of *homo sapiens*. Unqualified cultural and historical relativism constitutes the other extreme answer, contending as in two apodictic declarations that "my own group aside, everything human is alien to me" [4] and that "socialization goes all the way down." [5] Most positions on the issue can be located along a continuum between these two polar extremes. Biologists and evolutionary psychologists traditionally fall closer to the hereditarian end, while historians and social scientists, most notably cultural anthropologists, stand closer to the environmentalist end.

The question of how a common human biology and the varying cultural content transmitted through socialization, primarily in the family, interact to produce both similarities among individuals and differences at the group level is not equivalent to the issue of the relative importance of heredity or environment though it is too often treated by sociologists and cultural anthropologists as if it were. Sociologists, cultural anthropologists, and "historicist thinkers" [6] have frequently repudiated the very term "human nature" on the assumption that "nature" necessarily implies "original" nature, or universal traits determined by heredity. Others, however, have used the concept to refer simply to any and all qualities possessed in common by humans without necessarily assuming any direct biological causation of those qualities. Both biology and the common experience of socialization may be the source of commonalties among human beings even if the cultural content of socialization—of, strictly speaking, "acculturation" as distinct from "socialization"—is subject to wide variation. How both common and individual biological endowments interact with socialization within a particular family is central to the explanation of the individuality of persons as well as to differences at the group level and is the main subject of psychoanalytic therapy and of academic personality psychology in which both biology and socialization/acculturation are treated as variables.

2. The source and nature of individual deviation from social norms can also be regarded as an eternal question of social theory. It might be seen as a subset of the first question except for the fact that all of the forces of social control, from informal social disapproval to the established institutions of laws, courts, and prisons—are necessarily involved in considering deviance which therefore goes well beyond a primary focus on individual differences as such. Opposi-

tional deviant "subcultures" rely on the same forces. Culture is not what George Homans once called a "social mold" turning out individuals who are identical copies of one another, but most variation among individuals falls well within the conforming limits imposed by social norms. All societies however contain deviants who violate its reigning normative prescriptions, as Durkheim indicated in his famous statement that "crime is a normal phenomenon." Inquiry into the source, nature, and social response to deviation is a universal theme of social theory.

3. A third eternal question in social theory is how the desires and interests of individual human beings are controlled and/or meshed with those of others to make possible the very existence of stable social relations. The problem posed by such a question would not exist were it not for the relative scarcity of the objects of human desire, which, as Hobbes clearly recognized, entails that "... if any two men desire the same thing, which nevertheless they cannot both enjoy, they become enemies... and endeavour to destroy or subdue one another." Marx foresaw the total elimination of competition and conflict over material goods only when the means of production had overcome economic scarcity by creating an "economy of abundance. Despite his excessive confidence in technology, this was a realistic recognition of the only conditions that might end competition and conflict in human society. Talcott Parsons called the potential for conflict engendered by scarcity "the problem of order" and credited Hobbes with having been the first thinker to have clearly articulated it in secular terms though he did not accept Hobbes's solution to the problem.[7] He is not alone in having characterized it as the fundamental question of social theory. Parsons's normative solution tended, however, to occlude both the tensions between individual and society, on the one hand, and between groups in large-scale, socially heterogeneous societies, on the other, that accounted for recognition of the problem in the first place, projecting like Durkheim before him both an oversocialized view of the individual and an overintegrated view of society. The problem of order clearly confronts any and all social groups from the "micro" level of the family and other primary groups to the "macro" level of whole societies and civilizations.

The solutions to it achieved through the socialization of individuals, and the separate and distinct solution of regulating and limiting group conflict in larger "macro" social units, as well as the general forms taken by individual and group resistance to the imperatives of social order, make up a major part of social theory and inquiry.

I have called the first, the social control of individual impulses, "the hobbesian question," following Parsons: the necessity for avoiding "perpetual war of every man against his neighbor," using lower-case for the proper name because no more than Parsons do I accept Hobbes's antisocial rather than merely asocial view of original human nature, nor his coercive authoritarian solution for overcoming the "war of all against all." [8] A protracted period of directed social learning, or *socialization*, provides the solution, never a total one, by shaping and domesticating the unformed, inchoate original endowments of human infants.

The complementary "problem of disorder" [9] might be dubbed "the marxian question:" how to avoid schism between mobilized groups in complex societies that risks tearing those societies apart in internecine conflict. [10] Here too the lower-case for the proper name connotes rejection both of the extreme priority Marx assigned to class conflict over other forms of group conflict, and of his projected overcoming of protracted conflict by a socialist revolution establishing a "classless" society that would almost by definition be conflict free, at least at the level of groups. The peaceful regulation of group conflicts, even their procedural institutionalization, "solves," though never totally, the marxian problem.

Parsons failed adequately to distinguish between the hobbesian question to which the socialization of individuals was the answer, and the marxian question of potential conflict between groups. He collapsed together, or at least appeared to do so, Hobbes's "war of all against all" and the war of group against group. So, in effect, did Durkheim in seeing individuals afflicted with the condition of anomie, or lack of guidance by social norms and values, as the negation of social order at the level of whole societies while ignoring the marxian possibility of schism between warring groups with conflicting norms and values.[11] Clearly, the marxian problem is endemic only to socially heterogeneous, multi-group societies in which social groups more inclusive than primary groups, including nuclear or extended families, exist; it is not a problem confronting simpler relatively un-differentiated "tribal" societies. The marxian problem of the risk of social disorder becomes a reality only when the hobbesian question has been resolved at the individual level, for only individuals who have been socialized are capable of forming social groups and identifying with their collective goals which may include opposition to other groups.

The hobbesian question as one aspect of "the problem of order" overlaps the first eternal question of the nature of human nature. It focuses selective attention on those "socially relevant" aspects of human nature, both cognitive and motivational, that render humans susceptible to socialization from the earliest smile response of small infants to the capacity to "take the role of the other" (Mead), or to achieve a "reciprocity of perspectives" (Alfred Schutz) with others both cognitively and in the emotional form of sympathetic and em-pathic identification (Freud).

4. A fourth eternal question is posed by the ubiquity of social change. Why are societies inherently subject to change? What are the predominant causes of change? What is the prime mover, the "locomotive of history" in Leon Trotsky's metaphor, or is there a single one? If, as in the case of social reality in general, particular historical transitions can only ultimately be understood in par-ticular terms, the general factors capable of initiating social change nevertheless are subject to assessment and enumeration: demo-graphic processes altering the size, distribution, and density of populations; technical innovations based on advances in practi-cal or scientific knowledge; the effect of technology on the geo-graphical environment altering the constraints it imposes or cre-ating new ones; the outcome of internal group conflict—the marxian problem once again—resulting in changing balances of power; new religious and political movements often inspired and led by charismatic prophets that may lead to social revolutions; the broader question of whether or not unique individuals (or "great men") exercise an influence on major historical events and processes; the effects on societies of exogenous events such as con-flict with or invasion by other societies, mass migrations, trade rela-

tions, cultural diffusion, and the impact of natural catastrophes and lesser changes.

Group conflict, a subject clearly falling within the provenance of sociology, implies that the groups at odds with each other are seeking social change in striving to "win" the struggle by subjugating or abolishing the opposing group. To this extent, emphasis on conflict is congruent with an interest in social change as was repeatedly affirmed in the confrontation that loomed large in American sociology in the last half of the previous century between so-called "consensus" theories linked to structural-functionalist preoccupation with social stability and integration, on the one hand, and "conflict" theories linked to versions of neo-Marxism, Weberianism, and a concern with historical change, on the other. Conflict, however, does not inherently imply the occurrence of change for it may result in deadlock, or in recurrent cycles in which the rivals alternate periods of relative dominance. The notion of "balance of power" which has mainly been elaborated in connection with international politics recognizes this, but it obviously lends itself to a wider application to any and all social groups engaged in conflict over their aims and interests.

The overall pattern and direction of social change has often been considered independently of the question of the source or causes of social change conceived of as the question of whether there was a general "meaning" to the course of human history at large. The very first self-described sociologists, Auguste Comte and Herbert Spencer, were identified with the philosophy of history, which was seen as the essence of sociology at least until the generation of Durkheim and Weber. As late as the early 1940s when I was a prospective major in the field, I recall being advised by a learned Austrian refugee in Canada of the unsoundness of sociology for vainly presuming to understand and even to predict the inherently unforseeable course of the historical future. That social change follows a linear developmental course from the simple to the complex, often interpreted evaluatively as "progress," was a major early theme, seizing upon in the latter half of the nineteenth-century parallels between Darwin's account of biological evolution and the social evolution of societies. An opposed view that earned wide credence after the disastrous wars and totalitarian regimes of the twentieth century saw social change as cyclical with societies and the larger unit of civilizations undergoing ages of growth and expansion succeeded by eras of decadence and decline. Robert Nisbet noted that both conceptions are metaphorical, based on analogies with the developmental stages undergone by plants and organisms and both long antedate Darwin in going back at least to the Greeks.[12] There is also the Marxist view of social change that combines linear direction with cyclical rises and falls to produce a spiral or, more accurately, a ratchet motion based on an analogy with "dialectical" logic, although Marx also used the embryological metaphor of a "new society formed in the womb of the old." I have argued elsewhere that there is a "left/right rhythm of democratic politics" conforming to such a ratchet movement that combines a linear "drift" to the left with cyclical rises and declines of the rival "left" and "right" political tendencies, although far from being a universal pattern of social change, this rhythm presupposes the historical context of universal suffrage in relatively stable democratic polities.[13]

In a version of my own argument in the first chapter of the present book, Nisbet maintained that "If 'unique events,' as they are called, are not amenable to the systematic needs of social theory, so much the worse for theory…whatever the demands of social theory, the first demands to be served are those of the social reality we find alone in the historical record." [14] His phrasing is abstract, but he presumably has in mind our "demands" for the explanation of historical particulars as such. He qualified this categorical view to the extent of acknowledging that comparative historical studies are worth undertaking in order to answer such general yet delimited questions as "under what conditions do revolutions occur?"—questions that are clearly distinct from efforts to subsume entire societies, even humanity as such, under the overarching umbrella of a universal developmental schema. Although Nisbet was one of a few declared "conservative" thinkers in sociology, his case for comparative historical studies was similar to the argument of Barrington Moore, Jr., the friend of Herbert Marcuse, whose views are discussed in the previous chapter and who was widely regarded as a political "radical." The comparative approach can be applied to all of the general causes of social change: demographic growth, technological innovation, the appeal of new religious and political prophecies, et al. Nor need one entirely rule out eternal curiosity about a possible overall pattern and direction of human history, although it is worth recalling that some years before the charge of "Eurocentrism" was regularly leveled at Western thinkers Nisbet had noted the specifically Hellenic provenance of the organic metaphor as the model for speculations about patterns and directions. This metaphor was indeed the primary target of criticism in his valuable book. In a later work, however, he himself wrote a history of the idea of progress and mounted a qualified defense of the idea.[15]

* * *

The eternal questions of social theory may be debated at their own level of generality in addition to providing Merton's general orientations and Blumer's sensitizing concepts in confronting historical particulars with the aim of fully understanding and explaining them. Generalizing social theory discussed in its own terms nevertheless presupposes a vast corpus of substantive knowledge of "the human variety" (Mills). Employed to provide an initial perspective on particulars that will yield only "local knowledge," [16] the answers to eternal questions at least illuminate our understanding by assimilating historical uniqueness to this corpus even if they do not function as scientific covering laws permitting explanation of particulars by deductive inference from them. The answers nevertheless may be perceived as providing a better "fit" with the preexisting corpus and to that extent they are congruent with empirical realities rather than simply amounting to arbitrary preferences.

Biographical and historical knowledge illuminates the conjunction and interaction of the "factors" producing the effects that interest us, but for the most part such knowledge has no predictive value whatever. It is our relation to this knowledge, the fact that it is self-knowledge, whether of particular individuals, particular societies, or of the course of human history, that differentiates it from the natural sciences where our interest in the particularity of the objects studied, while not always absent, is distinctly limited. It is this that accounts for the voluminous compendium of knowledge of particulars taught in the humanities and the absence of any counterpart to it in the natural sciences, as noted in the previous chapter.

Notes

1.   C. Wright Mills, *The Sociological Imagination* (New York: Oxford University Press, 1959), 59-61.
2.   Robert K. Merton, *Social Theory and Social Structure,* Revised and Enlarged Edition (New York: The Free Press, 1957), 87-89.
3.   Herbert Blumer, *Symbolic Interaction: Perspective and Methods* (Englewood Cliffs, NJ: PrenticeHall, 1969), 147-152. The passage is from an article originally published in 1954.
4.   R. Rosaldo cited by Robert B. Edgerton, *Sick Societies: Challenging the Myth of Primitive Harmony* (New York : The Free Press, 1992), 27.
5.   Richard Rorty, *Contingency, Irony, and Solidarity* (Cambridge and New York: Cambridge University Press, 1989), xiii, 177m
6.   Rorty, *Contingency, Irony, and Solidarity,* xiii.
7.   Talcott Parsons, *The Structure of Social Action* (New York: McGraw-Hill, 1937), 89-94.
8.   Dennis Wrong, *The Problem of Order: What Unites and Divides Society* (Cambridge, MA: Harvard   University Press, 1994), 14 –36.
9.   Lockwood puts the phrase in quotation marks in the subtitle of his *Solidarity and Schism: "The Problem of Disorder" in Durkheimian and Marxist Sociology* (Oxford: The Clarendon Press, 1992). He conceived of it as the counter-concept to Parsons's term.
10.   *The Problem of Order,* 202-243.
11.   Lockwood, *Solidarity and Schism,* 107-110.
12.   Robert Nisbet, *Social Change and History: Aspects of the Western Theory of Development* (New York: Oxford University Press, 1969), 15-61
13.   My fullest and most recently updated statement is in *The Modern Condition: Essays at Century's End* (Stanford, CA: Stanford University Press, 1998), 63-86.
14.   *Social Change and History,* 279.
15.   Robert Nisbet, *History of the Idea of Progress* (New York: Basic Books, 1980).
16.   Clifford Geertz, *Local Knowledge: Further Essays in Interpetive Anthropology* (New York: Basic Books, 1983).

4

The Symbolic Animal

The earliest human beings certainly noted the specific physical and behavioral qualities that distinguished them from other living creatures long before Aristotle identified "Reason" as the defining attribute, the *differentia specifica,* of humanity. The Darwinian definition of humans as simply another animal species evolved by natural selection—a hairless, fully bipedal ape with a recessive jaw and an enlarged cranial capacity—nevertheless continued to name the species by its distinctive mental capacities as *Homo sapiens,* literally, "man the wise one." Other mental and behavioral attributes have been singled out by various Western thinkers as critically differentiating humans beings from all other animals. In addition to reason, nine other traits have been prominently mentioned, many of them advanced as alternatives to the "rational man" definition. All of them are essentially subordinate to, or effects of, the human ability to create and reproduce symbols of the individual's real or imagined experience, as I shall argue in this chapter, borrowing its title from Ernst Cassirer who suggested it (in its Latin version) in preference to rationality as the defining human trait.[1] It is nevertheless worth enumerating and briefly discussing the ten capacities other than symbol-creating that various thinkers have identified as the *differentia specifica* of the species.

1. "The rational animal" was, following Aristotle, for a long time the most common designation, "rational" being synonymous with reason and intelligence and equated in contrast to instinct or habit with conceptual thought and reflection in advance of action. Yet it has always been obvious that thinking and action directed by it may

be in the ordinary understanding of any of these adjectives neither rational nor intelligent, nor wise. This venerable designation was presumed to name a highly desirable potentiality, or "higher" capacity, by no means understood to be universally realized by all humans at all times.

2. "The talking animal" has also been a widespread definition with speech or language seen as peculiarly human though more tentatively so than rationality since it is recognized that we may simply fail to perceive means of communication employed by lower animals. This also applies, to be sure, to whether or not they are capable of reflection and rationality, but this qualification has less often been noted, probably because "blind" instinct and unreflective habit in situations where both are clearly inappropriate often seem to characterize the behavior of lower animals under both natural, domesticated, and experimental conditions. The ability to communicate through speech beyond mere vocal signalling is indeed distinctive of humanity, but requires further interpretation as to what precisely it involves and how it is achieved in both the individual and the species.

3. "Mind" or "consciousness" has commonly been held to be essentially human without necessarily being identified with rationality though obviously closely related to it as in Descartes' famous *"cogito ergo sum,"* the same observations usually mustered in its support. Often consciousness is tacitly identified with "self-consciousness" as distinct from consciousness *tout simple,* specifying the "reflexivity" that enables both the physical and mental traits of the actor to become objects of her/his own consciousness to which only he/she has access. I have, accordingly, not listed "self-consciousness" as a separate attribute though it is analytically separable from consciousness as such.

4. "The moral animal:" that humans possess a "soul" endowed with "knowledge of good and evil" has been a central belief of Christian theology, as well as earlier in Greek thought, long linked to the conviction that humans have been "specially created" by an omnipotent deity and have despite physical resemblances little in common with other animals. That man is uniquely "the moral animal," however, has often been maintained in strictly secular and naturalis-

tic terms independent of any version of divine creationism, sometimes phrased as the only animal capable of "internalizing" norms as rules to guide its conduct.

5. Another very common definition of humanity is as *Homo faber,* or man the tool-maker, the animal that uses material instruments to supplement its own organs in adapting to its environment. Henri Bergson may have been the *first* to formulate this definition as a preferred alternative to the conventional imputation of rationality in *Homo sapiens.*[2] Since tools are material objects, their discovery in archaeological excavations has played a major role in efforts to infer the mental and/or linguistic capacities of early humans and proto-human hominids whose fossilized bones were found with them. This definition, if not the Latin label itself, was notoriously favored by Marx, although Hannah Arendt has argued that Marx was actually committed to the rather different notion of man as an *animal laborans* (man, the laboring animal), which falls short of naming what is distinctively human in contrast to both *animal rationale* and Bergson's *Homo faber,* the creator of artifacts. [3]

The concept of "tool" involves three aspects that to a degree are independently variable: tool-using, tool-making, and tool-keeping. Tool-using is found among the great apes and higher monkeys in their use of stones to crack nuts, sticks to knock down fruit from trees, and the like. Rubbing flints together to make fire (the ability to make fire itself sometimes identified as the major distinctively human practice), shatpening sticks, stones, and bones to make knives, and attaching them to handles to make spears and axes are classic examples of primitive tool-making revealed in the paleontological record. The effort required to fabricate such tools suggests that they were not intended for a single use but were kept as valuable objects. There is little evidence that apes and monkeys keep for future use the objects they may employ as instruments in their subsistence or defensive activities. The famous case of Sultan, the captive gorilla who, according to Wolfgang Koehler *inThe Mentality of Apes,* fitted together two hollowed bamboo poles with his back turned away from a bunch of bananas he had previously been vainly trying to reach, and then after a moment's apparent contemplation turned around and used the *pole* to knock down the bananas, has been widely cited as illustrating in combination at the primate level elementary forms of tool-using, tool-making, and reflective intelligence.[4] Sultan's performance was seen as exceptional because the fruit he desired was not in his visual field, whereas other apes used sticks as tools only when the fruit was in full view.

6. "The cultural animal:" social anthropologists and sociologists dating back even before Alfred Kroeber's coinage of "superorganic," have long insisted that "culture," defined comprehensively as a socially, intergenerationally transmitted aggregate of habits of thinking, feeling, and acting, is uniquely human. It has been easy to show, as numerous accounts attest, that many, even most, lower mammals transmit at least some learned habits to other members of their species, most often as parents to their offspring, and this applies even to habits adapted to the special environments peculiar to animals kept as pets or in zoos, making for a diversity of animal "cultures" or at least "proto-cultures." Yet the volume of what is socially transmitted and the extent of dependence on it is so vastly greater for humans than for even their nearest primate relatives that a difference in degree credibly lends itself to being regarded as a difference in kind despite the unmistakable presence of more overlaps and continuities than in the case of the other listed criteria of the human. Some writers in their very definition of culture specify "socially learned by means of symbolic transmission," which makes culture in effect secondary to symbol-making as a marker of the distinctively human. Primitive forms of tool-making and indirect evidence of limited communicative signat1ing in hominid fossil remains have been designated as examples of a "paleoculture" less than equivalent to the full-fledged culture of early *Homo sapiens.*[6] How long it may have taken after the species had fully evolved biologically for the emergence of what may be designated as true culture is still a matter of debate among archaeologists and paleontologists.

7. "The time-binding animal: " this was the label favored by Alfred Korzybski in his monumental *Science and Sanity,* the book credited with the creation of "semantics" as a new intellectual discipline, fashionable early in the past century but today largely forgotten. Korzybski saw language as the human capacity that made possible

the conscious orientation of humans simultaneously to past, present, and future. Yet, curiously, he singled out this particular effect of language rather than language itself as the defining attribute of the species despite his primary focus on the relation between words and the realities they signified. Humans lived in an experiential world that included the past and future as well as the present whereas animals were able only to respond to their immediate situation, although their responses had, of course, been shaped by past experience and had future effects. Atbough Korzybski stressed the time-binding effect of linguistic consciousness, the use of language is also space-binding in enabling human beings to orient themselves to contemporary but spatially distant events and situations; "time-space-distanciation" (in Giddens' useful phrase) is a distinctive property of human consciousness.

8. *"Homo pictor"*: the philosopher Hans Jonas treated image-making or representation as a distinctive criterion of the human. He used it, however, in a rather special sense, not at all arguing that it was prior in time or significance to language or symbol-making but rather that the discovery of created images of objects in the environment would to an alien observer serve as instant and irrefutable proof of the presence of thinking, symbolizing creatures. As alien observers, Jonas adduced both hypothetical creatures with human mental capacities from other planets and archaeologists who discovered in tneir excavations sucn artifacts as the Aurignacian cave drawings. His argument was that even more than tools or hearths these drawings would provide immediate and indisputable evidence of the presence of *creatures* possessed offully human capacities and dispositiorn.

9. "The neurotic animal": Nietzsche referred to "the disease called man.. . the result of a violent breaking from his animal past..." He insisted that only humans were caught up in the conflict that resulted from the "terrible bulwarks, with which the social organization protected itself against the old instincts of freedom..." [9] Norman O. Brown borrowed Nietzsche's designation for the first chapter of his brilliant psychoanalytic interpretation of history, *Life Against Death.* [10] Herbert Marcuse presented a view similar to Brown's in his earlier, more abstract and theoretical *Eros and Civilization* [11] Freud himself obviously assumed that the mental pro-

cesses he discovered and analyzed were peculiarly human, presupposing the symbolizing capacities, both conscious and unconscious, that constituted the human mind, although he also postulated presymbolic motivations present in the unsocialized human infant and traced their development from infancy to adulthood.

10. "The death-conscious animal:" Existentialist thinkers have emphasized that human beings are the only animals conscious of the fact that they are mortal. They have made this awareness central. to their definition of man. Arendt, Jonas, and Marcuse were all three students of Martin Heidegger, generally regarded as the founding father of existentialism; their fellow-German refugee philosopher, Cassirer, engaged in a famous debate with.Heidegger in Switzerland in the 1920s. All of them saw themselves as engaged in the intellectual enterprise that became known as "philosophical anthropology."

Six of these attributes refer to human cognitive capacities, three to cognitive linked to motor capacities, and only one, "the neurotic animal," bears on motivation, at least indirectly. To characterize man as the "symbolic animal" is to single out a uniquely human cognitive capacity that underlies and is presupposed by all the cognitive attributes enumerated above in addition to shaping fundamentally from an early age human. emotional, motor, and motivational performances and capabilities. A complete account of human nature must obviously encompass cognitive, emotional, motor, and motivational capacities and dispositions how they interact, grow, and change in the course of the growth of personality. For this reason, an.exclusive focus on the symbolic falls short of constituting a full social psychology. George Herbert Mead is conventionally named by sociologists as the father of the "school" of "symbolic interactionism" seen as founded by Herbert Blumer who substituted "symbolic interaction" for Mead's "symbolic communication." Mead, however, was primarily a philosopher rather than a social psychologist or sociologist and his chief concern was the resolution of several traditional philosophical issues, such as the mind-body problem, the basic properties of human consciousness, and the *differentia specifica* of man compared to the other animals (he had studied in Germany and was certainly familiar with the tradition known as philosophical anthropology, different though his American pragmatism was from the Heideggerian background of Arendt, Jonas, and Marcuse.) Mead succeeded, I believe, as no one had before him or has since in isolating.and formulating just how man's symhol-making.capacity operates to bring into existence "mind, self, and society, the three entities enumerated in the title of his most famous (though posthumously published) work.[12]

Mead's essential contribution was his demonstration that the self as a reflexive object of consciousness is constituted by language with its duality of common reference to the actions of both ego and others. Social interaction, the basic subject matter of sociology, is therefore built into the very core of human consciousness. No wonder sociologists so fully embraced Mead. Mead's approach not only establishes a link to recent Saussurian structuralist thought with its conception of linguistic models that shape consciousness, but it was an effort—a succesful one, I believe—to refute Kant's pessimistic statement that "It is altogther beyond our powers to explain how it should be possible that *I*, the thinking subject, can be the object of perception to myself, able to distinguish myself from myself."[13] Mead similarly asked "How can an individual get outside himself (experientially) in such a way as to become an object to himself?"[14] Yet unlike Kant he believed he could answer this question. The question suggests that *self*-consciousness, not just consciousness as such, is distinctively human, posing special additional problems of understanding. Mead (like William James before him) had studied in Germany, was influenced by the neo-Kantians, and was certainly familiar with Kant's question. He insisted that "the self" was "a cognitive phenomenon,"[15] which implies that a person's attitudes and emotions towards her/his self to be phenomena of a different order presupposing the self's existence as an object of consciousness. As such a reflexive object, the self may become the object of the full range of attitudes and emotions towards any perceived object, as we recognize in such reflexive formulations as self-hate, self-glorification, self-judgment, and the like. If to overcome Kant's asserted impossibility of explaining self-consciousness is not to advance a full social psychology, Mead succeeded nevertheless in showing that self-consciousness is the product of symbolic communication.

A plurality of individuals in a common situation learns to associate the same sounds, Mead's "vocal gestures," with the same objects and events, such as food, weapons, caves, rain, fire. Such objects and events include the bodies and actions of the individuals themselves. As in the case of other higher animals, the vocal gestures of early humans functioned as signs or signals in social interaction. Humans are "babbling animals" and when both other people and the objects and events signified were absent they produced the sounds now associated with those objects and events. The sounds came to *mean*, "call up" in Mead's phrase, the absent objects and events, constituting what Mead called "significant symbols," the components of true language and of "mind." A necessary condition for this to occur is human possession of a brain and nervous system capable of "delayed response": humans do not instantly react with overt behavior to the symbolic vocal or subvocal (when individuals are alone) gestures they produce or hear spoken by others. Orientation to spatially and temporally distant circumstances—Giddens' "time-space distanciation"—results. This is the source of the human "time-binding"and complementary "space-binding" capacity involved in reflection, or thought in advance of action. In conformity to the maxim that "ontogeny recapitulates phylogeny," Mead regarded the process by which language originated among early humans and the child's learning of language as broadly similar, although he unsurprisingly drew almost exclusively on the latter for examples. I have added a few interpretive suggestions, some inevitably speculative, in the present account.

Mead's central idea was that to become a significant symbol conveying meaning the vocal gesture must at least covertly arouse in its maker the same response it arouses in the other to whom it is directed or who hears it. This creates common meanings in the minds of both and need not involve any active response, as Mead perhaps did not make as clear as he might have. Vocalization is able to achieve this, Mead insisted, because a sound is heard as the same whether spoken by an individual or by another; the vocal-auditory equipment of the human species makes fine phonetic discriminations possible: Mead laid great stress on this as a special property of vocalization. Therefore, when produced by an individual as a signal in social interaction, a sound arouses in the producer the same tendency the actual or potential response conveys; that is, the same meaning that he/she sought to arouse in the individual to whom it was directed, including, as I have noted, shared meanings in the absence of any overt action. This is the central proposition of Mead's explanation of the capacity to "take the role of the other" which he sees as the foundation of mind, self, and human society in its full richness and complexity. Although he refers sometimes to a "language of hands" and facial expressions,[16] he neglects to note that a person's manual movements and those of others are perceived as virtually the same because of the projection of the arms in front of the face and the distinctive five-fingered shape of the hand. It is not surprising, therefore, that a fully developed manual sign language has become an alternative to vocal language for deaf mutes and that manual gestures serve as a spontaneous makeshift means of communication for people who lack a common spoken language. Movements of the hands in apparent imitation of others occur in infants as early as their reproduction of similar sounds, the infant having witnessed its own random hand movements just as it has heard its own babbling voice. Some anthropologists indeed believe that early man developed a manual language before acquiring a vocal one, although it must inevitably have been much less complex and more limited in vocabulary.

But how do these processes generate a self? Mead addresses himself to this question in the third section of *Mind, Self, and Society.* The process by which the same sounds come to symbolize for a group the same objects and events in the environment is more readily understandable than how an individual's own acts and the observed acts of others, which are experienced quite differently, come to be symbolized as the same, Mead observed in a 1914 lecture rejecting "imitation" as an all-purpose explanation of the similar behavior of different individuals, "We are always affected by any process, but the affect of walking is not the same as seeing another person walking: this identity is to be found in the vocal and in the pantomimic gestures.[17] The establishment of identity is even more problematical for thoughts and feelings which are accessible only to a person's "private" consciousness. That other people have thoughts, feelings, and motives similar to one's own is an inference rather than something directly observed or experienced. Yet observation of others and their actions precedes awareness of the self as an object, as a "me" with the same general attributes as other people thus becoming an internalized object with which it is possible to interact as one interacts with others in the latent, internalized "conversation" with self that constitutes thinking. This is the essence of Mead's theory. He strongly emphasized in arguing against any form of solipsism this fundamental link between self and others with the perception of others coming first. His insistence on such a link is, of course, what has made him especially appealing to sociologists, also, morally and politically, to celebrants of community anxious to repudiate excesses of "privatism" and individualism, as well as to mourners over the human condition seeking at least some limit to what Joyce called "the soul's incurable loneliness." Sartre's distinction between the *pour-soi* and the *en-soi* is virtually equivalent to Mead's distinction between the "I" and the "me," although Sartre saw this as a painful, anxiety-provoking feature of human consciousness because of the gap between the two—the realm of "nothingness" he called it— whereas Mead's preoccupation was with the emergence of reflexive consciousness from more elementary behavioral responses, hence his "social behaviorism."

"Our symbols are all universals," Mead contended, "You cannot say anything that has any meaning at all that is absolutely particular; anything you say that has any meaning at all is universal."[19] Ensembles of universals can, however, be formed to describe particulars. Language, as linguistics scholars like Chomsky and Pinker have insisted, also contains an "elaborate structure" of rules for combining its constituent symbols: The ability to combine them in regular ways may depend on the specific neural structure of the human brain even if Chomsky's contested theories of an innate programming for generative grammar are rejected. The realities of the world, however, always consist of "absolutely particular" totalities, which is why realization of the unsurpassable gap between words and things can come as a painful metaphysical shock, as for Roquentin in Sartre's novel *La Nausée*. Mystics who claim to have achieved a unique awareness of ultimate reality have also typically described their visions as "unutterable" and "incommunicable."

Language as a means of symbolic communication originates as a response to the environment, as action on and interaction with a segment of it, namely, other people. Man is a "symbolic animal" because his capacity to symbolize, to endow his own gestures with meanings shared with others, is part of his adaptation to his environmental situation, whatever the labyrnthine, sometimes maladaptive lengths, to which this capacity maybe carried. In addition to consisting of universal symbols that make possible time-space distanciation, language also allows for the description of particulars even if it never quite matches or exhausts their ultimate particularity. The complex rules for combining symbols allow for such a variety of combinations that all of us have said things that were never said before or since, although the components of our statements are all universals. As for the subjects of our discourse, our interest in human beings and their societies is often in their very particularity and historicity rather than in subsuming them under universal or general categories. Social theory therefore at its best constitutes a kind of dialectic, a shuttling between the universal and the particular, between the transhistorical and the historical.

I shall conclude by indicating the relation between symbolizing and the ten attributes singled out as distinctively human that I listed at the beginning of this chapter: "Mind" is the self-stimulation by subvocal "gestures" originally acquired through overt symbolic communication with others ("speech" or "'language"). It possesses at least the potentiality of "rationality" and is capable of evoking temporally ("time-binding") and spatially absent events and objects (combined as "time-space distanciation"), an inevitable awareness of mortality ("death-consciousness"), self-judgment by general abstract norms or standards ("morality"), and the conception and creation of ways of supplementing adaptive organs of the body ("tool-using" and "tool-making"). It also makes possible the frequent painful simultaneous presence of conflicting emotions and motives ("neurosis"). Image-making (*"Homo pictor"*) is an iconic form of symbolizimg. Symbolic communication greatly increases the content of what can be socially learned ("culture"). Hence the appropriateness of "the symbolic animal" to identify the fundamental *differentia specifica* of the species.

Notes

1. Ernst Cassirer, *An Essay on Man: An Introduction to a Philosophy of Human Culture,* Garden City, N.Y.: Doubleday Anchor Books, 1953, 44.
2. Henri Bergson, *Creative Evolution,* New York: The Modern Library, Random House, Inc., [1911], 1944, 153.
3. Hannah Arendt, *Tne Human Condition,* Chicago: University of Chicago Press, 1958, 98-99.
4. Wolfgang Kohler, *The Mentality of Apes* (London: Routledge, Kegan & Paul, 1936), 193.
5. See the critical compendium by A.L. Kroeber and Clyde Kluckhohn, *Culture: A Critical Review of Concepts and Definitibns* (New York: Vintage Books, Alfred A. Knopf, Inc. and Random House, Inc., 1963).
6. Adam Kuper, *The Chosen Primate: Human Nature and Cultural Diversity* (Cambridge, MA: Harvard University Press, 1994), 80.
7. Alfred Korzybski, *Science and Sanity* (Lancaster, PA: The International Non-Aristotelian Library Publishing Company, 1933).
8. Hans Jonas, "Homo Pictor and the Differentia of Man," *Social Research,* 29 (Summer, 1962), 201-220.
9. Friedrich Nietzsche, *The Philosophy of Nietzsche* (New York: The Modem Library, Random House, Inc., 1927), 702.
10. Norman O. Brown, *Life Against Death* (New York: The Modem Library, Random House, Inc., 1959).
11. Herbert Marcuse, *Eros and Civilization* (Boston: The Beacon Press, 1955).
12. George Herbert Mead, *Mind, Self, and Society* (Chicago: University of Chicago Press, 1934).
13. Quoted by Geoffrey Hawthorn, *Enlightenment & Despair: A History of Sociology* (Cambridge: Cambridge University Press, 1976), 32.
14. *Mind, Self, and Society,* 138.
15. *Mind, Self, and Society,* 173.
16. *Mind, Self, and Society,* 147.
17. George Herbert Mead, edited with an introduction by David L. Miller, *The Individual and the Social Self* (Chicago: University of Chicago Press, 1982), 61.
18. For Sartre this was a fundamental metaphysical distinction with Hegelian overtones that he applied to a great deal more than only to human consciousness.
19. *Mind, Self, and Society,* 146.

5

The Value Ambience of Social Theory

It is scarcely surprising that accounts of the social world should be almost universally closely related to evaluations of that world whether in the form of proposals to change it or counsels of submission to it in its existing form. Even thoroughly deterministic theories purporting to do for society what the physical sciences do for natural phenomena involve at least the implicit advocacy of acquiescence in the way things necessarily are, or must inevitably come to be if theories of social change are at issue. Such implied counsel presumes at the very least the widespread presence among the unenlightened of belief, even if held to be illusory, in the partial reality of human agency that is lacking in the case of regularities in nature. "Praising" and "blaming" at the "micro" level of interpersonal relations presuppose that actors subject to moral judgment might have and could have acted differently although morality itself may be seen as entirely a social product. If the scientific effort to discover natural laws is ultimately justified by the possibility of accepting and conceivably manipulating them to human advantage, the abolition of the laws as distinct from their evasion or overcoming is not envisaged as a possibility. The most fatalistic social determinist, however, is aware that the constraints of social reality that he/she acknowledges are neither automatically nor universally recognized. That indeed is why it is considered worth advancing the argument that they are inevitably and unavoidably what they are and efforts to ignore them futile.

Social ideologies have in the modern era tended to supplant religions as the most comprehensive worldviews linking the true and the good as existential statements with normative prescriptions purportedly congruent with them. Those of a messianic thrust demand-ing total allegiance, frequently oriented towards the future and/or towards conflict with perceived enemies, have unsurprisingly been characterized as "secular religions." Insofar as they claim to be based on the findings of science, they possess the quality that Hannah Arendt called "scientificality" which stands in the same relation to actual science as "religiosity" to genuine religious belief. This does not apply, or at least not in the same way, to normative demands that presume the almost unlimited power of human agency. Such max-ims as "where there's a will there's a way," "if at first you don't succeed, try, try again," "anything is possible," or "we can do the possible, the impossible will take us a little while longer," if under-stood literally, express belief in a nearly total voluntarism. Such a view is obviously inconsistent with a deterministic conception of social reality. Yet presumably even the most thoroughgoing fatal-ism, including belief that everything in the world is dictated by the will of an omnipotent deity, would not be articulated unless its propo-nents thought there were people needing to be convinced of the utter futility of efforts to change things. That such a view is self-contradic-tory insofar as it implies the freedom of people so persuaded to desist from such efforts has often been argued. On the other hand, even a radical voluntarism recognizes a reality that exists and has been formed independently of the actor, limited though it may be to the world of nature including the constants of human biology. This limitation obvi-ously applies to individual actors confronting social reality, but it also applies to the social world that is a collective product of human actions despite the fact that many, perhaps most actions, both collective and individual, have unintended as well as intended consequences.

Social theories as well as ideologies largely fall between the two extreme poles of unconstrained voluntarism and total social-histori-cal inevitabilism; virtually all of them can be located at some point along a continuum from one extreme pole to the other. Indeed, their major aim is often to discover and articulate precisely *how* voluntarism and determinism combine to shape social-historical ex-perience. Classical economists often spoke of "iron laws" govern-ing economic activities (and Marx was one of their number in this respect), but those "laws" actually were conceived of as effects of the universal human desire to lower costs and increase gains in ex-changing goods and services. Contemporary social theorists who invoke the dichotomy of "structure" and "agency" recognize their interaction in the production of the social world, although one may dislike the pomposity and often talisman-like invocation of those terms themselves.

Inevitabilist social theories may be employed to justify conserva-tive, progressive, or radical valuations of the social order. Sometimes this is forgotten because extreme voluntarism appears to suggest that the autonomy of human agency means that anything is possible, that the world could be made over in the image of exalted ideals if only there were enough people willing to strive to do so. There is there-fore an apparent link between a stress on agency and the aim of chang-ing the world in some far-reaching way. There is moreover an equally plausible link between insistence that "there is no alternative" to the status quo (attributed to Margaret Thatcher by her critics as "TINA") and conservatism. And belief in what has been called "the inevita-bility of gradualism" is congruent with a theory of incremental change in a progressive direction. Yet popular brands of conservatism, radical-ism, or progressivism may see the stability of existing institutions, the imagination of desirable reforms, and/or full-fledged utopian "alter-native societies" as primarily the projects of far-sighted leaders, even "great men" of prophetic vision; both conformity to the status quo and ardent desire for change may be regarded as based on freely given consent. These are clearly versions of voluntarism.

Their explicit combination of determinism and voluntarism con-tributed powerfully to elevating Marxism and Freudianism to pre-eminent status as modern (or modernist?) social theories. At the in-dividual level, the goal of Freudian therapy is the discovery and overcoming of unconsciously determined motivations by restoring self-control and freedom of action to the conscious individual ego. At the collective level, Marxism is the most durable of determinist social evolutionary theories, asserting the inevitability of radical so-cial transformation and the futility of opposing it. Yet vulgar anti-Marxists have long claimed that Marxist insistence on the inevita-bility of socialism contradicts the advocacy of revolution as the means of bringing it about. That Marxism in contrast to other and earlier theories of social evolution foresaw a thoroughgoing break with the past brought about by purposeful collective human agency in the form of social revolution, seemed to render it vulnerable to such criticism for logical inconsistency. But Marxism was also a theory of *how* certain collective human motivations would emerge under specified conditions in the form of commitment to revolutionary agency. Subtle readings have detected "two Marxisms" striving to synthesize determinism and voluntarism while differing in emphasizing the priority of one or the other.[1] Marx's belief that universal proletarian class-consciousness would adopt a revolutionary form was mistaken, but his concern with the collective motivations of classes and historical actors is what makes him a sociologist going beyond the limits of narrowly economic theorizing. "Freedom is the recognition of necessity," an aphorism of Comte's adopted by and often attributed to Marx or Engels, is an oxymoron appearing to combine voluntarism and determinism in implying that recognition is not inevitable.

The Leninist modification of Marxism by substituting a party of dedicated indocrinated revolutionaries intent on mobilizing the working class though not themselves recruited from it has been the most historically consequential version of Marxism, one clearly representing theoretical movement towards the voluntarist pole of the voluntarist-inevitabilist continuum. Lenin did not advance an explicit determinist theory of why certain intellectuals of bourgeois background would decide to support and promote proletarian revolution other than their being persuaded of the truth of the writings of Marx, Engels, and Plekhanov. This injects an unmistakably more salient "voluntarist" element into the historical process than is present in classical Marxism.

All social theories deny that anything at all might happen at just any time, that social change is utterly indeterminate, that "structure" exercises no constraint whatever on "agency." Even the most deterministic theories can be seen, as I have previously argued, as counselling submission, whether resigned or affirmative, to the inevitability of the present or of the future they may project. Since social reality is fragmented and heterogeneous, it is usually seen as containing different possibilities of future development within the constraints of its present form with ideologies grounded in social-historical theories arguing with passion for the actualization of a preferred alternative. Such advocacy constitutes the incorporation of at least a degree of agency into a conception of structural limitation on possibilities of development.

The notion that a "value-free" social science is even possible is nowadays mentioned only to be rejected and often derided. The term itself is a translation of Max Weber's *wertfrei*, but what he actually advocated was the necessity of a distinction between the *advocacy* of values and the understanding of the social world including the values prevailing in it, between "appraising" and "characterizing" values in W. G. Runciman's terms. [2] In German, *werturteilfrei*, or "value-judgment-free," more accurately renders what Weber prescribed for social science. Weber also argued that worthwhile social science must possess the property of *Wertbeziehung*, or relevance to values as it has usually been translated. This amounts essentially to an assertion of the difference between "significance" and "triviality" in social science without implying that any particular exemplar of the difference is universal. (Recall the dismissal in the 1950s by Barrington Moore, Jr. of research on male "sexual aggression" as a typical example of "triviality.") Weber, of course, took it for granted that social values were culturally and historically variable. Indeed, he did not limit values to ideal qualities of human conduct or models of the social order, but also identified what he called "historical individuals" as in themselves constituting values or objects of value: this particular person, nation, group, or institution is valued in and of itself rather than because it incarnates abstract ideal values.

The notion that any and all social theories are inextricably bound to moral or ideological views of the world they purport to describe and explain must nevertheless be rejected. It is certainly true that in an obvious sense all statements about human conduct center on the ends and goals human beings typically pursue: obtaining subsistence from nature, providing for other elementary biological needs, avoiding life-threatening accidents and ailments, establishing cooperative relations with at least some other people. The term "values" is often used so loosely as to encompass these universal activities whatever highly variable forms they may take in particular contexts.

In that sense "facts" and "values" are inescapably combined in all social theory, identifying at least minimally what is significant as distinct from what is trivial in conformity with Weber's requirement of value-relevance. Social research is not undertaken to discover, say, what proportion of the population engages in nosepicking, sleeps on the right or left side of the body, or crosses legs when sitting. Of course, new theories may contend that what was previously regarded as trivial and inconsequential is actually symptomatic of hidden major determinants of conduct, Freud's "psychopathology of everyday life" being the classical case in point.

Yet the claim that all social theories are shaped or at least profoundly influenced by prevailing historically transitory moralities and ideologies confined to the society or epoch in which they are propounded goes beyond the simple assumption of the universality of certain practical human ends. When "values" are distinguished from "interests," the former is used in a more restrictive sense than the inclusion of any and all objects of human striving. The debunking overtones of Marxism and Freudianism stem from their reduction of all cherished values into, respectively, routinized self-serving economic interests, whether individual or collective, and biologically based bodily motivations. In linking values to the interests of classes under particular political economies, Marxism is a version, if a broad one, of historical relativism, whereas Freudianism sees values as reflecting the universal constants of human nature though assuming variable cultural-historical forms.

The postmodernist canon denies that the social sciences are cumulatively progressive like the natural sciences, insisting that they are indissolubly tied to historically transitory sets of values ("ideologies") that have shaped "factual" understandings and interpretations of the social world. Values are seen by their holders as actually or potentially capable of realization in the conduct of individuals and thus at least to that extent imply *some* conception of the nature of human nature and of the opportunities and constraints to which it is subject in society. If particular values are culturally/historically relative, so may be the conceptions of human nature and social life that they assert or assume though this does not *necessarily* follow. Extreme versions of cultural relativism and historicism postulate that culturally/historically specific values and/or interests shape all cognition. Cognition and valuation are seen as inextricably tied together. "Ideology" as a concept embraces both values and the understandings of the world invoked to justify them. Both are also covered by the term "worldview," which does not carry the invidious overtones that have come, at least since the debate in the 1960s over "the end of ideology," to cling to "ideology." "Worldview," whether or not it is contracted into a single word, is a translation of *Weltanschauung,* which paradoxically —possibly because the word is German and evokes the Nazis—also occasionally carries negative overtones as connoting a dogmatic, totalistic view of everything similar to the invidious nuances of "ideology."

Claims for the cultural-historical relativity of worldviews pose the familiar problem of distinguishing between universals and particulars in human experience. The problem is raised with reference to values alone when they are regarded as a separate realm independent of the empirical world of man and society, apart from in the minmal sense noted above. The most far-reaching Western tolerance of "diversity" and "multiculturalism" is unlikely to extend to acceptance of cannibalism, human sacrifice, physical torture, terrorism, slavery or genocide as colourful examples of the variability of cultures.[3] The effort to define minimal "human rights" amounts to a striving to establish a universal moral standard analogous to the search for generalizations empirically applicable to all men and societies.

Since values are seen as actually motivating most human conduct and as often held inflexibly with strong emotions mustered in their support, subject only to very general tests of experience, it is not surprising that they are so often believed to dominate empirical understanding of the world. This view in combination with recognition of their cultural/historical variability thus supports a near-total cultural-historical relativism. But it is not obvious that commitment to values as the ends or goals of action necessarily dictates, wishfully as it were, choice of the means or consideration of the conditions under which that action takes place. Ends, means, and conditions may be interdependent, but they are also partly independent of one another, which is why we are able to distinguish them as aspects of "the structure of social action." The same, of course, applies to the norms prescribing or proscribing the selection of particular ends and means, which was Parsons's major argument in his famous book. In principle, a particular understanding of the world might be regarded as prior to the values with which it is associated, as virtually dictating their content. The reverse, however, is more credible since values are held with greater passionate commitment than descriptions of the world though the two are often enough indissolubly combined.

If social and political ideologies had become "secular religions" supplanting for many allegiance to traditional religions, by the end of the twentieth century they too had become "gods that failed" no longer inspiring passionate commitments. The "end of ideology" was proclaimed by Daniel Bell as early as 1960.[4] His view was widely criticized and rejected to such an extent that the brief revival of political radicalism that followed often seemed to be partially willed by a wish to refute him.[5] From the perspective of several decades later, that revival now resembles a last effort to breathe life into Marxism and indeed into *any* vision of "socialism" as representing an attainable new society differing in vital respects from the existing social order. Nationalism, of course, survives, even flourishing in the wake of the decline of more universalist belief systems. German National Socialism can certainly be regarded as an extreme form of nationalism, but its racist and anti-democratic tenets and its effort to divert to its own advantage the positive value aura clinging to "socialism" made it into something more than the celebration of a particular people and its history independently of any general affirmation of their particular social and political institutions that is common to all forms of nationalism. This is attested to by the fact that it had imitators in other, non-Teutonic nations.[6]

Both the notions of "utopia" and of "revolution," born in the late Middle Ages and united as possible end and means of collective action in the seventeenth century, had by the beginning of the new millennium lost appeal to all but small minorities in Western countries and increasingly in the rest of the world.[7] The Soviet model of socialism had for some time disillusioned the vast majority of its former adherents—this was one of the conditions that induced and lent plausibility to Bell's notion—but the idea of a democratic socialism free of the incubus of the Soviet Union and its imitators played a role in the political ferment of the late sixties and early seventies. So widely had Soviet and even Chinese Communism been rejected and identified as totalitarian, that it remains surprising how completely and rapidly surviving Marxisms and socialisms have lost support since the collapse of the former and its satellites in 1989-91 and the increasing departure of the latter from a fully socialized economy. One speculates that the credibility of socialism depended to a greater extent than was fully acknowledged on the idea that Soviet Communism represented at least a kind of socialism in its state ownership of the means of production, a kind transformable into a different more desirable "democratic" and egalitarian form. The fullest early expression of this view was the doctrine of the Soviet Union's status as a "degenerated workers' state" that nevertheless rested on "unshaken economic fundaments" as Trotskyist foes of Stalin's dictatorship used to phrase it.[8] Soviet stagnation and ultimate collapse have evidently dealt a deathblow to the very idea of a planned economy that dispenses with price competition among independent producers. Nor is it any longer evident that the professed communist ideals of equality combined with collective decision-making remain inherently attractive, the ideals despite their perversion in practice accounting for the long survival in the past of the communist regimes. The rapid and largely nonviolent disintegration of those regimes in 1989-1991 seems to refute both the economic viability of state ownership and the attractiveness of "socialism" as an ideal. It was still possible before the collapse to separate the "end of idology," meaning a rigid, catechistic applied socioeoconomic doctrine, from the "end of utopia" (Russell Jacoby), meaning the conception of an ideal society believed to be attainable by political action.[9]

"Getting it right" may also be a prime value. A broad awareness of cultural variability, a far-ranging knowledge of the sheer diversity of values in human societies, may proscribe blindness or insensitivity to allowing one's own values to shape one's view of the world. Such awareness is certainly central to the credo of social scientists. The limitations of all social theories lie not so much in lack of objectivity deriving from strong moral or ideological convictions as in their incompleteness, restricted scope, and failure to envisage possibilities beyond those present in the existing historical record. What has never yet been seen on land or sea may nevertheless be a real possibility even if it remains no more than that.

Yet the most rigorously anti-ethnocentric aspirations to be "value-free" in social theory cannot help but reflect the existing level of knowledge and conceptual development in the social sciences themselves, which have their own only partially autonomous periodized history. Indeed this applies also to the physical sciences which pride themselves on being cumulative (that is, "progressive") bodies of knowledge independent of extrinsic influences. But this obvious limitation of perspective is not the equivalent of claiming that ideological commitment, or attachment to time and space-bound "tribal" values, inescapably dominate everyone's vision blinding them to any true assessment of social reality, even that of professional scholars and thinkers.

The most elaborate and far-reaching claim that any and all conceptions of social reality are unavoidably determined by the culture and power structure of the analyst's own society has been advanced by contemporary poststructuralists, most notably by Michel Foucault and his followers. [10] The "linguistic turn" in social thought has suggested a far deeper penetration of social constraints into language itself. This approach has usually had an affinity with an adversarial post-Marxist rhetoric preoccupied with inequalities of power, whether based on class, race, ethnicity, or gender. If the power of some groups over others is regarded as the most salient feature of society, and language is the primary medium of cultural expression and transmission, then language must inescapably reflect and reinforce social inequalities. It becomes both a major instrumentality and an effect of the exercise of power. All language in this view thus resembles George Orwell's "Newspeak" in *Nineteen Eighty-Four:* it cannot help but affirm the existing order and exclude the very possibility of even cherishing ideas critical of that order. As a "dominant discourse" it maintains the "ideological hegemony" of the already privileged by "foregrounding" them and their concerns while "marginalizing" subordinate or "subaltern" groups. Existing power relations penetrate the very core of human consciousness. Power relations are implicated in anything and everything that can be said, which makes everything "political" so that even the lack of specific reference to power and politics points to "silences in the text" that reveal a presence confirmed by its very absence. Not even Stalin went so far as this, contradicting it anticipatorily when in 1950 he intervened in a controversy over linguistics in the Soviet Union to insist that language at least was independent of class determination grounded in the economic "base."

Stalin makes an odd and unwelcome bedfellow. But I am in full agreement with the social historian Lawrence Stone when he wrote in the course of a controversy with Foucault: "Since man is a social animal, and since all social life involves some form of influence, molding, direction, or compulsion, the reduction of all social life to issues of power renders it almost impossible to make the fine intellectual, moral, and material distinctions necessary for any serious evaluation of change in history."[11] This conclusion, it is perhaps unnecessary to add, applies just as much to social order or stability as to social change.

Thus apart from periodization in the history of the social sciences itself, including whatever degree of cumulation they may achieve, it does not follow that any and all social science is time and space-bound by its social-historical context. One may concede that in contrast to the vaunted cumulations in the physical sciences, a special sensitivity is desirable and even necessary in the social sciences to minmize ethnocentrism in any of its forms. Conventionally, this is regarded as necessary because of the passionate emotional commitments with which beliefs in the proper conduct of fellow human beings and the shape of their social institutions are invested. Beliefs about natural phenomena are not usually held with comparable intensity though, of course, some at least may be linked to totalistic religious and ideological worldviews. There is also a lesser hiatus than in the natural sciences between systematic efforts to understand the social-historical world and the "common sense" embodied in the "ordinary language" of both the scholar-scientist and of his/her subjects of a different period or society. This is not simply the result of the putatively underdeveloped state of the social sciences in contrast to the natural sciences, but follows also from the fact that, extreme "reductionist" theories aside, social science must necessarily try to see the world from the subjective "point of view of the actor" (Parsons) as an intrinsic part of its explanatory task. Neologisms sometimes are coined in emulation of the natural sciences, and sometimes to eliminate the supposed contamination with values of ordinary language. To be sure, even the most magic-ridden and superstitious tribal society must possess a broadly accurate "common sense" understanding of its physical and biological environment as a condition of survival and the developed natural sciences do not negate such an understanding. These sciences may, however, in their findings and conceptual language depart radically from common sense. It is unlikely that this will ever be substantially the case in systematic studies of human consciousness and the societies in which it is embedded. Thus the avoidance of culturally relative value-based assumptions about them carries a special relevance for the social sciences even if it does not preclude relatively "objective" transcultural understanding.

Notes

1.   Alvin J. Gouldner, *The Two Marxisms: Contradictions and Abnormalities in the Development of Theory* (New York: The Seabury Press, 1980).
2.   W. G. Runciman, *A Treatise on Social Theory: The Methodology of Social Theory,* Volume One (Cambridge: Cambridge University Press, 1983), 304-341.
3.   Robert B. Edgerton, *Sick Societies: Challenging the Myth of Primitive Harmony*(New York: The Free Press), 1992.
4.   Daniel Bell, *The End of Ideology: On the Exhaustion of Political Ideas in the Fifties* (Glencoe, IL: The Free Press, 1960). The title appears in the book's epilogue; its chapters were originally articles published in 1951-59.
5.   As reported by Joseph Dorman, *Arguing the World: The New York Intellectuals in Their Own Words* (New York: The Free Press, 2000), 134-135.
6.   A valuable recent survey is Walter Laqueur, *Fascism: Past, Present, Future* (New York: Oxford University Press, 1996).
7.   Melvin J. Lasky, *Utopia and Revolution* (Chicago: University of Chicago Press, 1976).
8.   Trotsky used both phrases in urging his Fourth International followers not to support "capitalist" Finland when it was invaded by the Soviet Union in December, 1939. I remember as a fifteen-year old just converted to "socialism" stumbling upon his statement and the debate over the issue in the American Trotskyist organ *The New International* which led

to a split in the minuscule movement between the followers of James B. Cannon and of Max Shachtman who rejected Trotsky's position, characterizing the USSR as a new form of society that he labelled "bureaucratic collectivism." It turned out to be great "anticipatory socialization"(Merton's phrase) for my later encounter in New York City with Dwight Macdonald and his fellow ex-Shachtmanites

9.   Russell Jacoby, *The End of Utopia: Politics and Culture in an Age of Apathy* (New York: Basic Books, 1999). I attempted to dissociate the discredited concept of "ideology" from the idea of "utopia" in "Reflections on the End of Ideology," *Dissent,* 7 (Summer 1960, 201-205

10.   See especially Foucault's *Power/Knowledge: Selected Interviews and Other Writings* (New York: Pantheon Books, 1980).

11.   Lawrence Stone, "An Exchange with Michel Foucault," *New York Review of Books,* March 31, 1983, 44.

6

Art and Its Powers of Transcendence

Social theories advancing purportedly universal propositions may often overgeneralize from the particulars of the historical period in which they were created, as it has been the distinctive task of the subfield of the sociology of knowledge to demonstrate. Representational art reproduces concrete particulars, yet its creations that are most honoured by posterity carry an aura of transhistorical, even universal, significance altogether distinct from the purely technical innovations in the medium that may endow some of them with lasting interest. Critiques of social theory seek to relate its generalizations to the historically specific circumstances of their creation, even sometimes denying altogether their claims to generality; critiques of non-abstract artistic creations, on the other hand, seek out the wider meanings implicit in the concrete particulars they represent. Both approaches from opposite starting points involve a dialectic of the relation between universals, or at least far-reaching generalities, and time and space-bound historical particulars.

Some years ago I directed a graduate seminar on how to write sociology and assigned the class the task of writing a review of Kristin Luker's excellent *Abortion and the Politics of Motherhood.*[1] Inevitably, we were drawn into a discussion of the subject of the book, a vivid ethnographic study of women active in the anti-abortion movement that had come into being in the 1970s. Most of the students in the seminar were women, all of them committed feminists favoring without qualification the constitutional right to abortion affirmed in the 1973 Supreme Court decision. They expressed incredulity that any educated, thoughtful woman could, in contrast to Luker's mostly lower-class high school dropout subjects, be anything but in favor of abortion on demand. I demurred, remarking that in the not-so-distant-past before the feminist resurgence of the early 1970s many if not most women had often felt considerable ambivalence towards the very idea of abortion. Suddenly there popped into my head Hemingway's story "Hills Like White Elephants" and I immediately asked if anyone in the class had read it. No one had. Yet the story exemplifies the unique capacity of literature to capture the emotional depths of human situations in a way that social science can never match.

Hemingway regarded "Hills Like White Elephants" as one of the half-dozen short stories he thought his best. V.S. Pritchett chose it to represent Hemingway in his 1981 edited anthology *The Oxford Book of Short Stories*. Critics and biographers have agreed that it is one of his best, more than one describing it as a masterpiece. The story consists largely of conversation between a young American man and woman drinking in the café of a railway station in the valley of the Ebro in Spain while waiting to catch the express train from Barcelona to Madrid. The man repeatedly assures the woman that the surgical experience she is about to undergo will not be much of an ordeal and will not affect their relationship and the love they have for one another. She answers evasively and tries to change the subject, dwelling on her earlier observation that the distant hills look like white elephants. When he persists in his reassurances, she finally entreats him "Will you please please please please please please please stop talking!" Abortion is never mentioned, although early in the story the man insists that "it's really an awfully simple operation...they just let the air in and then it's all perfectly natural." The story ends after he has moved their bags in preparation for the train's imminent arrival and the woman smiles at him and tells him she "feels fine."

Several commentators on this story have described it as the account of a man hectoring, even bullying, a reluctant woman who is his lover into having an abortion. The fullest such version is by Jeffrey Meyers, one of Hemingway's more recent biographers.[2] Milan Kundera has written a devastating line-by-line demolition of Meyers's description of the story, selecting it as an example of "how kitsch-making interpretation kills off works of art." Meyers, Kundera argues, converts the story into a "moral lesson" in which the woman by resisting abortion stands for all that is good—nature, life, instinct, altruism—while the man represents egoism, abstract rationality, unimaginative literal-mindedness.[3] If Kundera had known more about American life, he might have pointed out that Meyers occasionally seems to echo the rhetoric of the anti-abortion "pro-life" movement in current American politics. Kundera is particularly hard on Meyers'successive comparisons of the story to Dostoievsky, Kafka, the Bible, and Shakespeare. He then objects to a French translation of the title of the story as "paradise lost," pointing out that there is no such implication in the story.

Kundera emphasizes the story's sparseness, its lack of any information about the couple's past, even whether or not they are married, as well as the absence of authorial psychological interpretation of the characters. The story, however, fully reveals Hemingway's justly famous psychological subtlety and does indeed not support the gross notion that the man is bullying the woman into doing something she really doesn't want to do. In assuring her that the operation will be a simple affair, the man is also seeking reassurance from her that it will have no lasting effect on their relationship. She appears anxious for a like assurance from him, although her reluctance about the abortion and her sense that things between them will never again be the same become evident in several later remarks tinged with bitterness. The story is so minimalist—to be guilty of anachronism in using a term that came into critical use much later—that it is subject to slightly different interpretations. Whether fear of the operation itself or regret over the loss of a baby accounts for the woman's mixed feelings is not clear, although it is hinted that she may perceive the man as obtuse for seeming to assume that it must be the former. Yet the claim that the man is bullying her into doing something against her will ignores indications that they have already agreed on the abortion and are taking the train to travel somewhere to have it performed. (Abortions were probably not easy to obtain in Catholic Spain in the 1920s). That the woman is nevertheless unhappy about the planned abortion is unmistakable and her declaration at the end that she "feels fine" is readily interpreted as ringing false.

My students hadn't read the story, but if they had they conceivably might have regarded it as presenting the benighted attitudes prevailing in the past before the recent feminist dispensation, though I may be doing them an injustice in suggesting this. Quite possibly, however, at least some of them might have reacted against the suggestion that the woman's attitude was based on regret over the prospective loss of a baby, seeing it as reflecting a dominant male assumption, in this case Hemingway's, that women were primarily "natural" childbearers. What makes the story meaningful to later generations, even a masterpiece as Kundera is not alone in describing it? Does not its capturing of the attitudes towards abortion of two presumably unmarried (though this is not stated) young upper middle-class Americans living abroad in the first half of the twentieth century condemn it to datedness and even incomprehension in the future? The literary classics are great because they succeed in transcending historical limits to create identifications with people living in very different times and places. This alone, as none other than Karl Marx recognized, refutes any total historical or cultural relativism in confirming the existence of at least elements of a common human nature present in quite different circumstances. However, might not Hemingway's very mastery of indirection in which far more is intimated than is ever directly suggested in the characters' talk or in the author's account of the setting work against such identifications? This possibility raises starkly the whole issue of universal meaning in relation to historical particularity as it applies to literature and to art in general as well as the issue of a common human nature.

To begin with, there is aesthetic tradition itself. In one of the most famous statements in his most famous critical essay, T.S. Eliot wrote of poetry, "…the historical sense involves a perception, not only of the pastness of the past, but of its presence; the historical sense compels a man to write not merely with his own generation in his bones, but with a feeling that the whole of the literature of Europe from Homer and within it the whole of the literature of his own country has a simultaneous existence and composes a simultaneous order." [4] Literary scholars have long devoted themselves to seeking out the "influence" of past writers on a particular work; indeed, such a task was once virtually definitive of literary scholarship itself. Kundera flays Meyers for pretentiousness in claiming to discern traces of the very greatest literary classics in "Hills Like White Elephants." Perhaps it is far-fetched to have suggesed as Meyers did that Hemingway was, intentionally or not, echoing King Lear's repetition of "never" in the woman's reiteration of "please," but there can be little doubt that Raymond Carver, a short story writer often compared to Hemingway, was remembering Hemingway's character when he entitled one of his own best-known stories "Will You Please be Quiet, Please?" also chosen as the title for his first collection of stories. The phrase is uttered by a man to his wife when he has returned home with a cut face from a mugging after a whole night's disappearance following her telling him of her single act of sexual infidelity a few years earlier.

The influence of earlier on later works has been dubbed "intertextuality" by contemporary theorists of literature. Extreme deconstructionists have argued that it is the sole content of texts and that attempts to compare them with a supposed nontextual reality is a metaphysical error. But if the claim that *everything* in human experience is a text, or at least can only be apprehended as a text, is accepted, then why should characters in a work of fiction not be compared with "real" people and written representations with an external reality? Why if all the world is a text is this any different from comparing written texts with other written texts, even though actual people and their situations are doubtless much more complex and indecipherable than written texts. I have never understood why deconstructionist logic rules out traditional efforts to estimate the degree to which literary works are "true to life" no matter what metaphysical assumptions one may hold about the ultimate nature of life or reality. If this is accepted, the notion of "intertextuality" need not be understood as referring solely to the influence of other texts unrelated to the realities the texts represent even if one adheres to the deconstructionist canon.

Hemingway has often been described as a painterly writer who was as much influenced by Gertrude Stein's pioneering collection of modern painters as by her tutelage on writing. He said early in his career that he wanted to achieve in literature the effects that Cézanne had achieved in painting. When I first read the opening paragraph of another of Hemingway's own favorite stories, "In Another Country, "I felt a surge of exhilaration at the thought that dusk in Milan in the autumn of 1918, the street lights coming on and a cold wind blowing off the Alps ruffling the fur of the dead animals hanging outside the butcher shops, would now be remembered forever. I did not know when I read the story years after it had been written about a time before I was born in a city I have never visited that this passage had become widely praised as exemplary prose by English professors in the classroom.[5] There is also the famous opening chapter of *A Farewell to Arms* in which the summer dust stirred up by the boots of the marching soldiers coats the leaves of the olive trees and the winter rain blackens the branches of the chesnut trees. And there is the equally famous passage in "Big Two-Hearted River" describing the flowing stream forming a convex surface against the log supports of the bridge while the trout below hold themselves with their waving fins against the current above the pebbly bottom. I would also include the view through the kitchen backdoor of ore barges moving slowly across the blue lake from "Up in Michigan." Nature, to be sure, is the dominant presence in all of these cases.

Eliot's assertion referred to poetry and there is a sense in which intertextuality is most salient in poetry, the essence of which is the originality, harmony, and incantatory beauty of the words themselves. It does not seem quite proper to apply the term to painting, although if all human perceptions are mediated by language, with nothing existing outside the text as Derrida contended, then it would presumably be entirely legitimate to do so. More than any other artistic medium non-abstract painting represents the world in its full concrete particularity. Yet as Simon Schama concludes of Rembrandt, "he will always speak across the centuries to those for whom art might be something other than the quest for ideal forms..." [6] There is a poem by John Updike in which after describing two Hopper paintings he ends with the lines :

> We have been here before. The slanting light,
> the woman alone and held amid the planes
> of paint by some mysterious witness we're

invited to breathe beside. The sewing girl,
the letter. Hopper is saying "*I am Vermeer.*" [7]

Thus the "intertextuality" of painting.

In another visual medium, when I am asked what my favorite movie is, my answer is a not particularly well-known French movie of the 1970s, *The Lacemaker.* The movie tells the story of a young woman, played by Isabelle Huppert, who works in a hairdressing salon in an undistinguished Paris suburb. For her annual vacation she goes one summer to the resort of Deauville where she meets the scion of a wealthy family owning an estate there. They fall in love. He is a student at the Sorbonne and on their return to Paris they continue the relationship. She becomes pregnant, has a miscarriage, and suffers a breakdown. Unable or unwilling to marry her, he visits her in the sanitarium where she is confined. He leaves and the movie ends with the camera moving in for a Vermeer-like closeup of Huppert's lovely, vacant, immobile face, and a voice intones "She might have been a lacemaker." It was a brilliant stroke of the director to have named the movie after the title of a famous Vermeer canvas, but it was not the only thing that moved me deeply. There is a scene where the student takes his girlfriend to a party with his fellow-students; they are jabbering away animatedly about politics and catching a word she asks him "What does it mean, dialectic?" He haltingly tries to explain it to her. The entire scene captures superbly the whole experience of the 1960s student revolts, and not only in France. The movie's story is, of course, the eternal Romeo-and-Juliet theme of a socially mismatched and ill-fated love. But for me at least, what especially endows it with power and greatness is its combination of painterly intertextuality, historical specificity, and an eternal theme. Hemingway's greatest stories, of which "Hills Like White Elephants" is certainly one, amply exhibit this same combination.

What accounts for the immense attraction Hopper's paintings have for so many people? I heard the poet Mark Strand in a lecture he later expanded into a small book say that many of the paintings reminded him of what he had seen as a child in the 1940s from the back seat of his parents' car driving around the country in the Northeast. Hopper's several paintings of scenes observed from railroad tracks evoke for me what I saw from Pullman berths in the 1930s when my family travelled each summer by overnight train from Washington, D.C. to Toronto, Canada. But there is more to the appeal of the paintings, Strand goes on to argue, than nostalgic recollection and he tries to define the "pictorial strategies...that locate the viewer in a virtual space where the influence and availability of feeling predominate."[8] I once tacked a number of postcards of Hopper paintings on the wall of my university office. One day I was visited on business by a young woman on the administrative staff; as she left, she paused, glanced at the cards, pointed to one of them, and said "I do love that painting so!" It was "Early Sunday Morning" depicting a row of empty stores facing the street, including a barbershop with a barber pole in front of it, with a second storey façade of smooth red stone, the windows with half-drawn blinds and closed lace curtains. It is one of the most famous Hopper paintings, my own favorite, and was in 1931 just the second to be acquired by a museum, the most expensive purchase yet of the new Whitney Museum's acquisitions. It is a simple almost photographic reproduction, according to Hopper himself "almost a literal translation of Seventh Avenue,"[9] although I have always identified it with Brooklyn where there are many architecturally similar rows of houses, conventionally described as "brownstones," doubtless because I once lived there in such a row. But there is a strange quality to this "cityscape" that I can only think of as a metaphysical aura somehow conveying a sense of the beingness of Being, or perhaps the presence, more likely the absence, of God. (Hopper claimed that someone else added the titular reference to Sunday.) If this sounds too portentous and grandiloquent, it might be that Hopper succeeds in presenting commonplace, inevitably time-bound human artifacts *sub specie aeternitatus* —a gaunt frame house in an obsolete architectural style, a drugstore advertising Ex-Lax, hotel lobbies with furniture of "faded thirties plush" (Updike), automats and cloche hats.

Yet there are surely some works of art that capture a contemporary situation that is bound to be transitory without communicating this sense of eternal brooding over the passing scene. They are neverthelesss too good to be depreciated as merely "dated," which might in the case of literature be understood as meaning that their creators did not adequately grasp the transitoriness of their depictions but wrote in a subhistorical spirit in the false belief that they were communicating something that at least in part transcended the limits of time and place. An obvious example that escapes these limitations is the fiction of John O'Hara, as does that of a rather different writer, Mary McCarthy. A more stylized minimalist example in which there is something marvellous, even miraculous, about the exact brief rendition of turns of phrase and mundane sights and scenes is Evan Connell, Jr.'s novel *Mrs. Bridge*, which was made into a movie, and its later less successful sequel *Mr. Bridge*, both describing upper middle-class life in the Midwest in the 1920s and 30s. Perhaps it is the vividness and convincing accuracy of the recreation of an entire world of experience in nothing but words that suffices to provide the aura that endows such works with lasting value. In the case of painting, the most concretely representational of the arts, more than sheer "photographic realism" is required if they are to endure as ackowledged masterpieces, as is also true, for that matter, of photography as an art. Nor, as previously mentioned, is it a matter of innovative technique in manipulating the medium. Masterpieces must project some suggestion of the depths and possibilities of human experience that is more than simply accurate representation of the details of what they depict.

The successful couching of the universal in the particular as the defining criterion of great literature is a version of the blend of the transhistorical and the historical that is also the essence of the sociological imagination in Mills's famous phrase. Both are exercises of imagination, which alone is capable, in Hannah Arendt's words, of "eventually catch[ing] at least a glimpse of the always frightening light of truth," though "theory" trafficks in "interminable dialogue and 'vicious circles'" while literature creates imagined representations of particular human lives. [10] Proust called his multi-volume masterpiece *In Search of Lost Time* and strove to recapture the taste of pastries once served at tea time and the muffled sounds from downstairs after he had been sent to bed as a child. Joyce said he wanted it to be possible to reconstruct from his writings Dublin as it was in 1905, streets, shops, and all. Why is *Ulysses* considered the greatest novel in English of the twentieth century while an old tourist brochure on the sights and scenes of Dublin is not regarded as literature at all?

At the end of *Lives of Girls and Women*, her "portrait of the artist as a young woman," Alice Munro writes:

> Voracious and misguided as Uncle Craig out at Jenkin's Bend, writing his history, I would want to write things down.
>
> I wanted to make lists. A list of all the stores and businesses going up and down the main street and who owned them, a list of family names, names on the tombstones in the cemetary and any inscriptions underneath, a list of the titles of movies that played at the Lyceum Theatre from 1938 to 1950, roughly speaking. Names of the streets and the patterns they lay in.
>
> The hope of accuracy we bring to such tasks is crazy, heart breaking. And no list could hold what I wanted, for what I wanted was every last thing, every layer of speech and thought, stroke of light on bark or walls, every smell, pothole, pain, crack, delusion, held still and held together—radiant, everlasting. [11]

This passage is Munro's declaration of her commitment to artistic creation, her equivalent of Joyce's "I go forth to forge in the smithy of my soul the uncreated conscience of my race." Why is *Lives of Girls and Women* a great novel, entirely comparable to those of Proust and Joyce, while her Uncle Craig's compendium of information about the town is a bore that Munro's autobiographical fictional heroine destroys after his death? The intimation of the universal in the particular is surely part of the answer: the vivid evocation of actual experience projecting a sense of its timeless possibility yet unmistakably locating it in time, space, and history, an echo of Nietzsche's myth of eternal recurrence. The case is not different, I want to suggest, for the best social theory, which starts, however, with abstract, general statements and moves on to their embodiment in particulars, also marked by unique traits, the reverse of Munro's creative starting-point. The best literature and social theory manifest an imaginative sensing of a link between relatively abstract general truths as elements of experience and the thoroughly concrete particulars of a given time and place, fitting the two together in a symbolic synthetic representation that is evocatively suggestive in literature and explicitly formulated in social theory.

Writing on the epistemology of the social sciences, W.G. Runciman distinguishes *reportage, description, explanation,* and *evaluation.* The second and third of these evoke the famous *Erklaren/ Verstehen* controversy of the German *Methodenstreit* in the first decade of the twentieth century that has been waged in varying terms ever since by philosophers and methodologists of social science.[12] By "reportage," Runciman means simply the bare factual, "behavioristic" recording of the events and individual actions that are the subject matter of particular social science inquiries. "Description" goes beyond this, requiring the communication of what it feels like as a human experience to experience the relevant events and situations. This is clearly the distinctive realm of art and literature. Description also entails the understanding of meaning, or *Verstehen,* as a necessary, even unavoidable, feature of social science, insisted on by so many critics of the application of a "natural science model" to human affairs, thus radically differentiating the methodology of social science from that of all of the physical sciences with marginal exceptions for the study of some behavior of the higher animals. Atoms, stars, and cells cannot report (at least so far as we know) what motivates them or what it feels like to be an atom, star, or cell—if indeed motives and feelings have any meaning at all when imputed to these entities. Understanding human action encompasses both the actor's cognitive awareness of a situation and her/his ensuing intention to act, including attendant emotions, with at least intimations of the intention's rootedness in deeper more recurrent motivations.

Accordingly, description of a human action trancending the mere recording of overt behavior must center on the point of view of the actor, on her/his perceptions, feelings, and intentions in relation to the concrete situation in all its particularity since all human action takes place in such a situation and is oriented to it. But the perceptions, beliefs, goals, intentions, feelings, and deeper motives of other people, can only be "understood" by beings for whom these mental-emotional phenomena also make up the content of their own "subjective" experience. At the same time, without implying a thoroughly gratuitous "free will," the explanation of any action requires direct reference to the actor's understanding and purposive intention in the absence of which it might have been quite different or not have taken place at all. This is the actor's "agency" in bringing about a particular outcome. Even if convinced that he/she "had no choice" but to act in a given way, the action is still a motivated, intended reaction to the perception of an external situation rather than a quasi-automatic response to a stimulus. One cannot therefore draw a hard and fast line between understanding (*Verstehen*) and causal explanation (*Erklaren*): they blend into one another, each at least partially entailing the other.[13] This was the prime contention of the critics of the "covering law" model of historical explanation summarized in a previous chapter.[14] "Structure," at least as perceived by the actor, is clearly not ruled out as a feature of the actor's situation in explaining an action, but "agency"—the actor's motivated and intentional decision to act in a given way—is included, implying that the actor *could*, whatever he/she may think, have acted differently or not at all. Good literature even when depicting people and situations alien to the reader grounds them in recognizably common subjective human experience.

What is required for full explanation is showing the linkage between structural factors and the actor's "dynamic assessment" (MacIver) of the situation and the subsequent intentional action. This was what Parsons argued in insisting that the "point of view of the actor," her/his ends and means as well as external conditions, had to play the major role in any and all explanations of the "structure of social action," making "the means-ends schema" the equivalent in his view of mass, motion, and volume in physics.[15] Parsons's argument was directed against the behaviorist psychology that was fashionable at the time he wrote, a polemical orientation that was ignored by his later critics who focused on his analytically separable claim that consensual social norms regulated the selection of means and ends to charge him with conservatism for neglecting the ubiquitous ambiguity and conflict over norms in complex advanced societies. At roughly the same time, Robert MacIver argued that "social causation" (the title of his book) required primary consideration of the "dynamic assessment" of the actor, defined as the mental synthesis the actor makes of ends, means, and perceived situation in deciding to act.[16] MacIver too was polemicizing against behaviorist as well as against other determinist psychologies and sociologies that failed to identify the actor's intention as at least the immediate (or "effective") cause of action. Though it was not a term he used himself, George Herbert Mead was called by his posthumous editor a "social behaviorist" because his starting-point was generic animal behavior in response to stimuli from the environment. But, as I have shown in chapter 4, Mead's achievement was to demonstrate how human symbolic communication creates an internal mental environment in which the individual, in effect, conditions herself/himself by the latent, "interiorized" processs ("thinking") of presenting the self with symbolic representations of experience. Thus Mead showed exactly how the intentional actions so insisted upon as essential to understanding human conduct by Parsons and MacIver developed out of the more primitive, generic forms of acquired stimulus-response behavior common to both humans and those lower animals capable of learning.

To the extent that this is so, the fashionable dichotomy of "structure" and "agency" in contemporary social theory is in itself inadequate and misleading. Explicit recognition of the concrete singularity of both the actor's subjective orientation and the recurrent ("structural") external features of the situation in which the action takes places must be combined in interpretive understanding. This blend of evocative description and explanation of human experience is also present in literature; successful literature may be defined by its achieved implicit fusion of the richly particular with intimated overtones of the universal, of the "eternal questions" arising out of experience that social theory strives systematically to answer. If theory starts with the universal, or at least the general, and reasons from it to the particular, literature and representational art starts with the concretely particular and creates at least an aura or intimation of the universal or general.

7

The Historical, the Transhistorical, and the Subhistorical

The word "history" and its derivatives, of which the *American College Dictionary* lists no less than nine, have a fairly wide range of more or less diverse meanings. To begin with, "history" denotes both the object studied and the study of it, "historiography" distinguishing between them by denoting only the latter. Feminists once insisted on complementing the root noun with "herstory" and it is certainly true that the experience of women was generally neglected by past historians, but the prefix of classical derivation is only incidentally the same as the possessive form of the male pronoun and was never intended to be gender-specific. The suffix derives from the Latin *storia*, meaning a story, a narrative sequence of events, and is commonly so used in ordinary speech. When referring to the scholarly field of study, "history" is generally understood to connote *past* events and situations. The term "contemporary history, " though widely used, has at least a faintly oxymoronic ring, as does Theodore Draper's title *A Present of Things Past*. It is often said of present events and situations that "history will decide" or "judge" their significance, meaning that future assessments of their eventual long-range consequences are indeterminate, knowable only after enough time has elapsed for them to have been fully absorbed into the past. All this is obvious enough.

As for diverse meanings, "history" and the "historical" may variously stand for the first term in several sets of binary verbal pairs: past versus present and/or future, particular as opposed to universal or at least general, time and the temporal contrasted with space and the spatial, the temporal against the timeless or eternal, and, often in

85

sociology, social change in contrast to stability or persistence. The contrast between the actual or the "concrete" and the abstract is a variant of the particular/universal contrast, with abstract implying not just the general or universal as such but detachment or "abstraction" from a particular larger context as in Mills's derogation of survey research as "abstracted empiricism" contrasted with his affirmation of Karl Korsch's "principle of historical specificity."[2] When used to mean the particular or the unique, "history" and "historical" connote that which is confined in time and implicitly in space, limited to a specific context for which the contrary is the universal or at least the general. Used in this way, the reference may be not only to a temporal narrative sequence of events but to institutions, cultural beliefs, or entire types of society or "social system" that have endured over considerable periods in the past yet do so no longer, such as slavery (an institution), belief in the idea of progress, or feudalism (a social system). Obviously, these designations rest on broad generalizations about the behavior of individuals and groups, although they are restricted as generalizations within given temporal and spatial parameters. Statements about them may take the same logical form as universal statements, for example, "All early factory workers worked long hours for low wages," yet they refer to what have been called "closed classes," that is, classes for which it would be at least in principle possible to enumerate every single member.

Analytic philosophers of history have contrasted such closed classes with "open" classes, equating the latter with universals, that is, with the ongoing reproduction with no prospective termination of individual members of the class.[3] The contrast they intend to draw is between historical statements and scientific laws. But such statements as, for example, "Americans take a reverential attitude towards their Constitution," also refer to an open class although it will almost certainly become closed at some time in the future since neither "America" as a nation nor its Constitution can be assumed to survive forever. There are, of course, categories of Americans to whom the generalization does not apply, for example, many political science and law professors, but that is not the issue here, which is simply that neither the document, the attitude towards it, nor even the nation itself are likely to survive indefinitely, or at least for as long as the human species or the planet endures. Such generalizations in that they are confined to time and space-bound particulars will eventually become "merely historical" in the sense of having existed only in the past though they may not yet have been superseded by social change and thus remain temporarily open classes. This fits many, even most, sociological generalizations, although they assume the logical form of generalizations about open classes in denoting classes that are indeterminately open. The notion that history deals with the past and sociology with the present is to this extent warranted. Such generalizations about contemporary phenomena might be described as "subhistorical" without any invidious implication. "Prehistorical" or "ahistorical" are possible alternatives, but the former (as "prehistoric") is regularly used to denote the period antedating the existence of written records of human life and the latter has been often been employed invidiously by critics.

The major difference between the natural and the social sciences lies in what Martha Nussbaum has called "the priority of the particular" to describe the latter.[4] Her phrase is perhaps preferable to my own "the persistence of the particular," chosen for this book's title, as well as to "historicity" and to Bent Flyvbjerg's "context-dependence" as features of the social sciences meaning essentially the same thing.[5] These alternative labels may too readily be taken to suggest that there is some substantive property of humanity and its works, the basic subject matter of the social sciences, that differentiates them from the realms studied by the natural sciences. There *is* of course such a difference insofar as human beings are determinedly particularizing creatures primarily oriented to the singular concrete contexts in which they find themselves. The difference this makes for the social sciences compared to the natural sciences, as I argued in earlier chapters, lies in *just what it is that we most want to know* about the two realms as implied by Nussbaum's "priority of the particular" which in no way denies that *all* phenomena possess both general and particular attributes. My choice of "persistence" does not, however, prejudge what it may be that we want to know about concrete events and situations, suggesting merely they cannot be understood in total separation from their particular context. The difference from the natural sciences lies in the perspective of the human observer rather than in the objects observed. Our interest in human affairs, as Nussbaum postulates, often gives priority to their particularity and reflects the uniquely human properties of mind and language; these properties are as conducive to *particularizing* as much as to *generalizing*, granting that our statements about particulars are ensembles of general concepts in the form of the symbols constituting language. The enormous "generative" potentialities of language makes it possible to describe particulars in verbal ensembles that, as Chomsky insisted, ensure that all of us have spoken or written sentences that have never been spoken or written before by anyone. The uniques ness of such sentences at the same time that they consist of words that are general in their symbolic reference nicely illustrates the synthesis of the general and the particular in human cognition.

As I argued at length in chapter 2, we are simply less interested most of the time in how, figuratively speaking, any two peas in a pod differ from one another. A correspondent to the *Times Literary Supplement* of February 28, 2003 criticized me for asserting that "every object... in the universe has aspects peculiar to it" and insisted that "every atom of carbon-12 is essentially the same as every other atom of carbon-12" which accounts for the difference between the physical sciences and the bio-social sciences. It may be a quibble on my part to respond by simply pointing out that two objects rather than one at the very least differ in their spatial location, but my claim was that our *interest* in nonhuman phenomena was not focused on their individuality. We are indifferent to whatever unique traits many—most—natural and material objects may possess beyond the common properties they share that make them serviceable to human purposes, acknowledging that sometimes we may cherish particular objects such as locks of hairs or faded flowers as durable momentoes of other people and social events. Knowledge of human affairs, on the other hand, involves what Anthony Giddens has called a "double hermeneutic": it consists usually of particularized interpetations of the usually particularized interpretations of its subjects that therefore fail to lend themselves to the standard natural scientific goals of generalization, prediction, and control. [6] Human beings in everyday social interaction also certainly presuppose, take for granted, general attributes possessed by their fellows most of which are sufficiently obvious at the level of common sense to have required no disciplined inquiry by specialists to establish their truth. Insofar as sociologists seek to summarize these attributes in the logical form of general propositions resembling those of the natural sciences, they are vulnerable to the charge, often still levelled at them by historians and humanists, that they are merely "elaborating the obvious." As Nietzsche noted, "What is general is often empty and banal," or at least is perceived as such.

I argued in chapter 2 that we usually want to know not merely the necessary conditions that precede the occurrence of particular events but the sufficient conditions as well. The former are inherently general in the sense that we know that their presence invariably precedes all individual occurrences of the event, but the conditions sufficing for the event to occur may be irreducibly particular, such as individual personalities, the event's location in a temporal narrative sequence, its larger historically specific situational context, and the like. This is putting it all very abstractly. But to illustrate by my earlier example of the sort of historical questions to which we seek answers, "Why and how did Hitler come to power?", the necessary conditions of acute social conflict, economic distress, recent national or at least collective humiliation, perceived external enemies and the like may, let us provisionally assume *always*, precede the coming to political power of aggressive, demagogic, authoritarian leaders in violation of traditional or established rules, but these by no means uncommon conditions have often enough been present without that result occurring. It is the particularity of the sufficient conditions, therefore, that need to be understood in order to account for the unique and unforeseen case of Hitler's ascension in 1933, for example, the senility of the nominal head of state, bitter political divisions on both the left and the right institutionalized by the party system, onorous reparations and territorial losses imposed by the wartime victors, ambiguous clauses in the Weimar constitution, the lingering effects of the Great Depression, Chancellor Schleicher's failure to ask for a lengthy adjournment of the Reichstag, and so on. [7]

The same applies to other preeminently "historical" questions such as "What were the causes of the First World War?" (the causes of the Second are sufficiently obvious to preclude scholarly exploration), "Who will win the coming election?.," "Will a particular national conflict over territory lead to peaceful negotiations or to armed conflict?.," "Why did the crime rate in a given society decline in one decade and increase in another?"

All of these questions except perhaps the last are examples of Fernand Braudel's *histoire evenementielle* in contrast to the trends and structures of his *longue durée.* [8] The social and economic history practiced by the *Annales* group bore a close resemblance to the subjects studied by sociologists: people's daily routines, their workaday beliefs, their demographic traits, and the like, for which statistics are inevitably a major source and method of investigation. Braudel's work and earlier examples of what came to be called "social history" stood in contrast to the "kings and battles" kind of recorded history as narrative in reaction against which sociology at least in part arose. Not only the distinction between past and present (between closed and open classes), but the very features of human life that sociologists studied were scarcely covered by historians and this was not owing solely to lack of access to reliable quantitative information about past social and economic situations as opposed to well-documented political and military events. Sociology promised to tell us something new about the forces shaping our everyday lives. It involved intimate "reflexive" self-knowledge in contrast to the then conventional topics of historical study. My father and grandfather were both academic historians who tried to dissuade me from studying this dubious new-fangled discipline, but the first book in sociology I ever read was the Lynds' *Middletown* which was on my father's own bookshelf and was much respected by him. The Lynds had no background in the academic sociology of their day and their book was introduced by a leading contemporary anthropologist who described it as "a pioneer attempt to deal with a sample American community after the manner of social anthopology."[9] This ethnographic aspect of many of the early sociological studies, including the researches conducted at the University of Chicago, was a major source of the field's initial appeal quite independently of any aspirations to emulate the natural sciences. Several of the pioneering American sociologists had been cultural anthropologists or, like Robert Park, journalists who had been posted in foreign countries.

In seeking to establish broad generalizations, sociologists have frequently conceptualized large-scale sequences of social change. In schematizing the changes accompanying the urban-industrial development of the West the earliest sociologists frequently assumed, or at least implied, that future changes in any and all parts of the world would duplicate the experience of the West. The early social evolutionists, most notably Comte, Spencer, and their followers, are the most salient examples of this version of Western historical ethnocentrism or "temperocentrism" as it has sometimes been called. Such generalizations are clearly not "transhistorical" in the sense of applying universally, that is, to any and all human societies. Later writers muted the idea that the succession of "stages" in Western development had been "inevitable" and were likely to be repeated in non-Western regions to the extent of constituting "laws" of social change comparable to those of nature, but they still often at least suggested that "underdeveloped" or "developing" areas could be expected to repeat much of the broad experience of the West.

By far the most famous stage theory of historical development is that of Marx and Engels, influential needless to say far beyond the ranks of academic social theorists. Marx and Engels postulated a transition from a "prehistorical primitive communism" and later "tribal" society to the historical sequence of ancient society, feudalism, and capitalism or "bourgeois society" to be succeeded in the future by a temporary stage of "socialism" eventuating finally in full "communism" that would bring history to an end. Each stage was defined by its economic "mode of production" with slaves, serfs, and proletarians, respectively, forming the vast majority of the population of the last three historical stages their revolts initiating through victorious "class struggle" the transition to the next stage. Marx and Engels acknowledged the existence of a separate "Asiatic mode of production" characterized by state authoritarianism ("Oriental Despotism") and to that extent they were less "Eurocentric" than their social evolutionist predecessors. The emergence after the Russian October Revolution of 1917 of regimes that abolished "capitalist" private ownership of the means of production and instituted state-directed industrialization, and the eventual collapse in 1989-91 of Soviet Communism and its satellite neighboring states, clearly made obsolete the Marxist schema. Even the survivng Communist societies of the Far East (and Cuba) have modified strict state control of their economies by "restoring" capitalist elements of private production and market exchange.

Both affirmers of capitalism and its critics have often conflated capitalism with a market economy as such. Yet markets are a much more widespread social phenomenon, virtually universal in societies with populations larger than a few hundred persons living above subsistence level that have achieved a stable division of labor in production. Adam Smith famously wrote that "the propensity to truck, barter, and exchange one thing for another" was a universal human disposition and he was surely right to have done so in identifying the disposition with the distinctively human capacities of "reason and speech." This passage from the *Wealth of Nations* is often cited dismissively as evidence of Smith's supposed identification of capitalism with human nature, but he makes no such identification, merely observing immediately after the most quoted passage that uniquely human attributes make exchange possible whereas dogs do not exchange bones.[10] The "free market," the "free" standing for relatively uncontrolled prices and unrestricted entry for both producers and consumers, cannot be equated with capitalism. Even when prices have been traditionally fixed or controlled by authorities the forces of supply and demand have given them at least some variability.

The eulogistic use of "free market" and "market economy," common since the collapse of Communism, has led to their being employed as affirmative labels even more commonly than that old favorite "free enterprise," reflecting the fact that "capitalism" has always tended to carry faintly pejorative implications. Ernest Gellner once wrote "Capitalism differs from God in one important respect: where it does not exist, no one will bother to invent it."[11] Fernand Braudel remarked that "The great thing about capitalism is that no one invented it."[12] Both writers meant that, in contrast to its alleged contraries "socialism" and "communism," capitalism had emerged as a decentralized, autonomous economy of production and exchange rather than as the result of centralized state directives or decrees, or as the achieved goal of a revolutionary social-political movement, even though the "ism" connotes something more historically specific than the general human disposition to exchange goods and services, the widespread existence of markets as institutions, and the at least partial interplay of supply and demand in determining the terms of exchange. Capitalism presupposes the existence of a market economy in which money is the major medium of exchange and goods are produced for sale by individuals or groups who own their means of production. It can properly be said to exist only when such ownership is restricted to a minority and nonowners survive by selling their labor, more specifically their labor-power, to the owners who also appropriate the proceeds of the sale of whatever the laborers produce. The existence of a market for labor and the clear separation of the wages earned by the laborers from the proceeds or profits accruing to the owners of the means of production from the sale of the product of labor is a definitive criterion of capitalism.

Sociology itself as a perspective and eventually an academic discipline virtually came into being as an effort to explain and document the social effects of what Karl Polanyi called the "great transformation" of Western European societies in the eighteenth and nineteenth centuries marked by the emergence of a fully capitalist economy.[13] The transition from "mechanical" to "organic solidarity" (Durkheim), from *Gemeinschaft* to *Gesellschaft* (Toennies), from a "traditional" to a "rational-legal" order (Weber), from social "organization" to "disorganization" (Thomas and Znaniecki) were major themes of the pioneering sociologists; in contrast to their predecessors Comte, Spencer, and Marx (more ambiguously in his case), they did not simply celebrate the transition as inevitable progress. "Loss of community" and of individual "identity" and the ensuing "quests" for them in complex, heterogeneous modern societies, and the appearance of new forms of social hierarchy and inequality have remained perennial themes of sociologists to the present day. Sociology might even be said to have originated in exploration of the underside, the negative effects, of the "great transformation."

When I was first a student of sociology in the 1940s and 50s just about everything that sociologists studied seemed to be accounted for by the degree of "urbanization and industrialization," a phrase that functioned as a kind of binary explanatory mantra. More recent analysts have ascribed "deindustrialization" and "postindustrialism" to the more economically advanced nations, referring not to any reversion to agrarian life but to the substitution of automated machinery and electronic technology for work formerly carried out by unskilled or semiskilled manual laborers assembled in large factories. "Modernization" as process and "modernity" as result, terms applied to much of the world now undergoing what has been called "globalization," have of late come to stand for changes once identified with capitalism and industrialism while "premodern," "modern," and more recently "postmodern," have become the most general classificatory rubrics for the societies of the world, though, especially in the case of the last, these labels originally referred to trends in literary and artistic fashion.

Even with regard to the limited and more or less precisely measurable example of population growth and distribution, the "theory of demographic transition" was thought to point to the future of areas that had yet to undergo it. Insofar as it constituted a "theory" rather than merely a summary description of Western experience,[14] it indeed correctly implied the general proposition that mortality levels were universally more susceptible to reduction than fertility levels, that people were more likely to welcome changes that would keep them alive longer and in better health than to adopt practices limiting the numbers of children they produced, in effect, choosing life over death. But even this restricted and entirely plausible transhistorical generalization does not simply result in the repetition in non-Western countries of the eighteenth- and nineteenth-century Western experience of the timing and duration of its phases of demographic change owing to enormous subsequent technological revolutions in medicine and public health practices (including methods of contraception), agriculture, and communications and transportation.

All of these changes on which sociology essentially cut its teeth are "macrohistorical" in Randall Collins's phrase rather than fully or truly "transhistorical," [15] applying universally. That distinguishes them from the universal propositions articulated as "laws of nature" in the physical sciences. If there has been much overgeneralization from historically singular phenomena in the social sciences, there has also been an exaggerated counter tendency identified with "postmodernism" to insist on the absolute particularity, uniqueness, and contingency of anything and everything. Any particular thing is, to be sure, at the very least a singular "event" located in the time-space continuum; it is what it is and not something else and is in that respect unique, but this hardly rules out its sharing common features with other events. If human beings habitually both *generalize* and *particularize,* they also, unsurprisingly, overgeneralize and overparticularize and the same is true of scholars. Experience consists both of the "irreducible particularities" emphasized in my first chapter and features shared with other experiences. In this sense the historical and the transhistorical are almost indissolubly blended together and much social interpretation involves an effort to disentangle them at least conceptually.

As for the category of the "subhistorical," this label might be applied to generalizations advanced without, unavoidably, any explicit indication of the still unknown and unknowable limits which their historical context will impose on just when and where they are likely to hold true. Inevitably, many, even most, generalizations made by sociologists about contemporary events and situations are of this kind since although they surely exist the relevant limits are clearly indeterminate, that is, cannot yet be determined. Indeed, such sociological generalizations are not usually thought to be valid *sub specie aeternitatus* though possessing their own significance and value in a strictly contemporary context. Inevitably, the bulk of ongoing sociological research falls and will always fall into this category.

As briefly suggested in an earlier chapter, "transhistorical" and "historical" are the equivalents of the universal and the particular as applied to human society. "Subhistorical," on the other hand, means no more than that particular events and situations cannot yet be clearly limited in their historical location and duration even when the events and situations in question are quite obviously historically specific with the continuity and duration of their recurrence yet to be determined by future developments. The notion that historians study the past and sociologists the present or contemporary is valid to this extent. The logical similarity that both true transhistorical generalizations and subhistorical generalizations about contemporary phenomena deal with open classes of events has provided a certain implicit but altogether misleading rationale for classifying sociology with the sciences and history with the humanities.

Sociologists have pioneered in the invention and the use of methods of direct observation that were for the most part not available to historians before at least the late nineteenth century. Once the generalizations arrived at by the use of these methods no longer apply to the contemporary world as a result of social change, they become entirely historical in content. They succeed nevertheless in enormously enhancing our knowledge and understanding of the social life of the past, creating whole new areas of study where previously sheer impressionism and reliance upon memoirs and literary sources had to suffice. Sociology has in this manner greatly broadened and deepened the content of historical study, especially study of the fairly recent past on which earlier sociologists had conducted research. In addition, historians have been motivated to seek out data roughly comparable to that of the sociologist however more limited in scope and reliability these data are bound to be. Whole new fields of historical study have come into being as a result.

It is tempting to rest content with the assertion that the sociologist tries to enumerate the universal or at least general *necessary* conditions for the occurrence and/or persistence of social events and situations while the historian seeks out the both the *sufficient* and the historically specific necessary conditions. The result is a synthesis of the general and the particular in the explanation of any given concrete social phenomenon. There is much truth in this even though it is too formulaic. The historian may be interested *only* in the concrete particulars, although her/his statements at a minimum necessarily consist of general concepts in the form of linguistic symbols. The sociologist on the other hand may be interested solely, or at least primarily, in subsuming particulars under general propositions of wider reference. The mindset of the sociologist is illustrated by a conversation I once had with a colleague who, after I had described this proposed book as an effort to show the interdependence of sociology and history, said rather condescendingly that the historian was, of course, concerned with "the details" of social phenomena, the implication being that these were essentially a minor, even trivial, focus of interest. Yet, especially in the practical or "existential " context of everyday life but also in collective "historical" contexts, it is the "details" in all their particularity and apparent contingency that puzzle us and call for explanation as to how they came to constitute sufficient conditions for the occurrence of a significant event. My example in chapter 2 of Hitler's coming to power is a typical if momentous historical example, for our interest in knowing how it came to happen in the supposedly advanced and enlightened society of early twentieth-century Germany is hardly satisfied by grouping it with other instances of the ascendancy of authoritarian dictators. Classifying an event as exemplifying a general proposition may indeed appease our curiosity and anxiety by assuring us of its "normality," but more often it is the very specificity of the sufficient conditions for it that we want to discover. That, I submit, to reiterate the point made in chapter 2, is why I, and not only I but many others, are more likely to turn first to historians or reliable journalists rather then to sociologists when trying to understand some significant contemporary phenomenon. That historians' explanations are vastly improved by the employment of Blumer's "sensitizing concepts" and Merton's "general orientations" is not to be doubted, but this does not contradict Nussbaum's "priority of the particular" as the dominant goal of their effort.

Notes

1.   Theodor Draper, *A Present of Things Past* (New Brunswick, NJ: Transaction Publishers, 2000).

2.   Mills mistakenly attributed this principle to Marx rather than to Korsch in *The Sociological Imagination* (New York: Oxford University Press, 1959), 149.

3.   W.H. Walsh, *Philosophy of History* (New York: Harper Torchbooks, 1960), 39-40; William Dray, *Laws and Explanation in History* (London: Oxford University Press, 1957), 46-49; Gordon Leff, *History and Social Theory*

(New York: Doubleday Anchor Books, 1971), 67, 83-85; J. H. Hexter, *Doing History* (Bloomington: Indiana University Press, 1971), 110; Alan Donagan, "Historical Explanation: The Popper-Hempel Theory Reconsidered," *History and Theory,* Vol. IV, No. 1, pp. 3-26.

4.   Martha C. Nussbaum, *Cultivating Humanity: A Classical Defense of Reform In Liberal Education* (Cambridge, MA: Harvard University Press, 1997),

5.   Bent Flybjverg, *Making Social Science Matter: Why Social Inquiry Fails and How It Can Succeed Again* (Cambridge: Cambridge University Press, 2001).

6.   Anthony Giddens, *The Constitution of Society* (Cambridge: The Polity Press, 1984).

7.   Henry Ashby Turner, Jr., *Hitler's Thirty Days to Power— January 1933* (Reading, Ma: Addison-Wesley Publishing Company, Inc., 1996), especially his closing chapter, "Determinacy, Contingency, and Responsibility," 163-183.

8.   See William H. McNeill's summary in *Mythistory and Other Essays* (Chicago: University of Chicago Press, 1986), chapter 10, "Fernand Braudel," 225-226.

9.   Robert S. Lynd and Helen Merrell Lynd, *Middletown: A Study in Modern American Culture* (New York: Harcourt, Brace & Company, Inc., 1929), vi.

10.   Adam Smith, *The Wealth of Nations* (New York: Random House, [1776] 1937), 171.

11.   Ernest Gellner, *Contemporary Thought and Politics* (London: Routledge & Kegan Paul, 1974), 183.

12.   Though sure of its authenticity, I cannot find the exact location of this quotation that certainly expresses Braudel's view in his *The Wheels of Commerce Civilization and Capitalism- 15th-18th Century*, Volume 2 (New York: Harper & Row, [1979], 1982 [English translation]), 231-373; or in his short book *Afterthoughts on Mterial Civilization and Capitalism* (Baltimore: The John Hopkins University Press), 1977.

13.   Karl Polanyi, *The Great Transformation* (New York: Rinehart & Company, 1944).

14.   Robert Gutman, "In Defense of Population Theory,"*American Sociological Review,* 25 (June, 1960), 332-339; Dennis H. Wrong, *Population and Society,* Fourth Edition (New York: Random House, 1977), 21-26.

15.   Randall Collins, *Macrohistory: Essays in the Sociology of the Long Run* (Stanford, CA: Stanford University Press, 1999).

8

Summary and Conclusion

My major aim in this book has been to insist that humans should be regarded as particularizing beings just as readily as the generalizing creatures capable of orienting themselves to new situations by reflecting on past experience that is usually regarded as the uniquely human attribute of "mind" or "consciousness." I have chosen to stress the "persistence" of the particular in order to affirm that the particulars with which human beings are preoccupied cannot be satisfactorily reduced to mere exemplifications of the general propositions or laws that modern science seeks to establish in the empirical realms it confronts. We almost invariably wish to know more about historical and biographical experiences and situations than what they have in common with others that are similar. Since my concern has been with the resistance of history and biography to encompassing explanatory generalizations, I have chosen to speak of the persistence rather than the "priority" of the particular though I fully agree with Martha Nussbaum's assertion of the latter.

Nussbaum's "priority" is her insistence that what we most urgently want to know are the causes and consequences of ensembles or temporal sequences of contingent situations or events. Generalizations from past experience may certainly help us gain this understanding. My prototype of such a question, reflecting my own generation's historical experience, was "Why and how did Hitler come to power in Germany in the 1930's?" Generalizations about the rise in the past of dictatorial "strong men" in crisis situations clearly cast light on the question but hardly exemplify reliable general laws while failing to designate the convergence of specific events that in their interaction and interdependence amounted to sufficient conditions for Hitler's ascendancy.

This priority and persistence of the particular and the contingent in what we most urgently want to know accounts for the fundamental difference between the natural and the social sciences. There are, of course, "eternal questions" concerning all human beings and their societies regardless of their diversity. Indeed, search for the major causes and sources of that diversity—whether culture, heredity, racial variation, the impact of particular historical events—is one such eternal question. But the answers to these questions while providing in Merton's words invaluable "general orientations" do not permit deductive inference to the causation of the particular sequences and ensembles we want most to understand. It is, of course, possible to note the distinctiveness of, and the particular narrative sequences undergone by, natural objects: histories of specific "rocks and rills and wooded hills"—and most certainly of individual members of other animal species. But our interest in them is usually based on their relation to human affairs (except perhaps in some instances of folklore and fairy tales personifying nature).

Language as a system of vocal and written symbols capable of almost infinite combinations and invention of new symbols is the foundation of humanity's unique mental powers. The "symbolic animal" is therefore the most appropriate name for the species in designating what is truly most distinctive about it. Rationality, mind, language, morality, time-space distanciation, tool-making, culture, psychological conflict or neurosis, the creation of images of the external world, and awareness of mortality have all been singled out by one or another thinker as constituting what is uniquely human, as the basic *differentia specifica* of the species. The possession of language, or—phrased more generally—of the capacity to symbolize the world, can be shown to be the foundation of all of the others. The "symbolic animal" is therefore the most appropriate label for the human species, encapsulating its behavioral uniqueness. Symbolizing involves the attachment of the same vocal, manual, or written signs to objects of the environment by a plurality of human individuals. Thus the production of a symbolic gesture by one person evokes the same image or "meaning" in the consciousness of another person hearing or witnessing it. This exemplifies what Mead meant by a "significant symbol." Combined with the capacity to delay any overt behavioral response, it is the foundation of humanity's enormous cognitive range and distinctiveness.

Descriptions and explanations of the social-historical world are usually closely related to evaluations of it whether seeking to change it or accepting it as a status quo. In the modern era social and political ideologies have tended to supplant religions in this respect. Popular brands of conservatism, radicalism, and progressivism have been embodied in Marxism, Leninism, and Freudianism at the level of the individual biography. Yet the notion that any and all social theories are veiled ideologies should be rejected. Social theories have, as Weber asserted, "value-relevance" and may yet be "value-judgment free;" that is, not concerned with directly promoting values. Several thinkers, notably Daniel Bell and Raymond Aron, reported the "end of ideology" as the twentieth century drew to a close. Yet conflicts over issues and ideas even if they do not form an integrated set amounting to a coherent ideology are bound to continue. Theories and propositions can be distinguished as historical (irreducibly particular), transhistorical (general), or subhistorical (of uncertain scope). My title "persistence of the particular" stresses the central value of the first of these. Sociology itself is the product of the "great transformation" (Polanyi) of Western Europe in the eighteenth and nineteenth centuries which was a major theme of the classical sociologists. The capacity to avoid standardized responses to new experience, whether based on instinct or ingrained habit, is the source of human creativity. Homo sapiens is as much a particularizing as a generalizing animal. That is the major theme of the book.

The capacity of human beings to act by choice in widely varying ways is taken for granted, a capacity lacking not only in natural objects but in most nonhuman animals. As previously noted, social and political ideologies have today largely replaced religions as worldviews conjoining the true and the good. They can be placed on a continuum from the most voluntaristic suggesting that "where there's a will there's a way" to the most deterministic that nevertheless still assumes some freedom of human agency. Most social theories combine elements of voluntarism and determinism, exemplified by Marxism at the collective level and Freudianism at the individual biographical. All social theories recognize that the preexisting structure of the social world limits at least minimally the power of human agency.

It has been fashionable in recent decades to deny that a "value-free" social science is even possible although such a claim is a distortion of Max Weber's more restricted recognition of the distinction between professing values and giving a "value-judgement free" account of the social world. Weber acknowledged, however, that significance in social science lies in its relevance to major values (*Wertbeziehung*). New theories may of course contend that what was previously considered trivial is actually replete with significance, Freud's *Psychopathology of Everyday Life* being the most obvious case in point. So-called "postmodernist" views deny that social science can ever be cumulatively progressive like the natural sciences, insisting that its propositions are inseparable from historically limited sets of values. Extreme versions of cultural relativism and historicism make analogous claims.

The responses to their environment of the lower animals are mostly invariable, dictated by instinct or ingrained habits and reflexes that are largely automatic in their operation. Higher animals are capable of learned responses that may be absolutely particularized, as in the attachments of domestic animals to individual persons and places. Dogs and cats taken away from their homes may find their way back over long distances they have never before traversed. But only human language synbols achieve a synthesis of the general and the particular; they are able to conceptualize the particular and thus retain it as memory in utterly novel combinations of commonplace words.

If science strives to move from the universal, or at least the general, to the concrete particular, art strives to invest concrete particulars with at least an aura of the universal or general. The greatest art endures because it successfully achieves this in becoming more than merely a reflection of its times. Works of art that do little but reflect their times are of course valued for their informative nature though also derogated as "dated." The greatest art, however, bridges the gap between the temporal and the universal creating empathy with people living in quite diverse times and places. If all the world is a text as argued by extreme deconstructionists, then comparing written texts with real experience is entirely legitimate as just another form of "intertextuality." The combination of intertextuality, accurate rendition of the historically particular, and intimations of universality virtually defines the greatest art. The successful synthesis of the universal and the particular also characterizes what C. Wright Mills called "the sociological imagination" though sociology in contrast to art starts with the universal and moves to the particular whereas art moves in the opposite direction.

The epistemology of the social sciences requires the union of the "objective" in the form of an accurate account of an actor's overt behavior and the "subjective" intentionality of his/her purpose in acting. Sociologists of the 1930s such as Talcott Parsons and Robert MacIver insisted on this in properly reacting against the fashionable "behaviorism" of the period that aimed at omitting any reference to subjective "mind" or "consciousness." "Understanding" the content of these was essential to any explanation of human nonreflexive conduct. George Herbert Mead, though calling himself a "social behaviorist," provided the most satisfactory explanation of how this union of "objective" overt behavior and "subjective" covert mentality came about. The source of human creativity is the capacity to overcome both instinct and/or ingrained habit by sharing with other individual human beings the association of common vocalizations to the same events and situations along with the neurological capacity to delay overt behavioral response while covertly subvocalizing or "internalizing" what had its origins in social interaction with others. In responding internally to his/her own subvocalizations the persons becomes, as it were, two persons, an "I" and a "me" in Mead's suggestive terms. An individual may produce vocalizations never before uttered that nevertheless consist of combinations of verbal symbols shared with others. The particular, that is, the novel combinations referring to particular objects, events, and situations, and the universal or general, that is, the separate verbal symbols connoting those objects, events, and situations, are thus synthesized.

The most enduring works of art from painting to literature and including the movies move from concrete particulars to project at least an aura of the universal or general. Such an aura accounts for their endurance, their avoidance of "datedness." Even works that are clearly limited to the time- and space-bound may endure because they project a real sense of human possibility rooted in common features of human nature. The literary classics succeed in creating identifications with people living in very different periods and places. Masterpieces must project some sense of depth and of the possibilities in human experience rather then just its details. They thus synthesize the particular and the universal or the historically specific and the transhistorical. The greatest art is defined by its success in blending intertextuality, historical specificity, and an aura of the eternal. As I have previously noted, Joyce, Proust, and Alice Munro are three great writers who achieve this synthesis, great *because* they achieve it. Science on the other hand strives to subsume the concrete particular under universal-general laws and propositions.

The distinction in the writings of social theorists betweeen the universal and the historically particular draws too sharp a dichotomy. "History" is usually understood to refer exclusively to the past although "contemporary history" has been used despite appearing to be an oxymoron. But "history" also is used in other dichotomies such as temporal/spatial, temporal/eternal, change/persistence, and concrete/abstract. "Historical" may refer not only to a series of events, a "story," but to institutions, beliefs, or entire societies that once existed but do so no longer. "Historical" usually refers to what phlosophers have called "closed classes" in which it would be at least hypothetically possible to list every individual member. "Open classes" on the other hand take the form of universal statements in referring to events and situations that are still in existence (e.g., "Americans elect their head of state."). Such statements characterize sociological generalizations about contemporary societies although their makers certainly do not believe that they will endure forever or at least as long as humanity endures. A distinction between the "historical" referring to the past, the "transhistorical" or universal-general, and the "subhistorical" referring to generalizations about contemporary societies but in no way carrying any invidious meaning better captures the different perspectives of social theorists and historians.

The philosopher Martha Nussbaum's invokes the phrase "the priority of the particular" to connote how the social sciences essentiallly differ from the natural sciences. She insists that detailed *particularizing* as much as *generalizing* is a basic property of human consciousness shaped by language. My analogous phrase the persistence of particular things" chosen as the title of this book is intended to suggest that the difference lies in what it is that the human observer most urgently wants to know about human affairs. The enormous "generative" potentialities of language stressed by Noam Chomsky makes possible the synthesis of the general and the particular. Knowledge of human affairs amounts to what Anthony Giddens called a "double hermeneutic," particularized interpretations of the usually particularized interpretations of its subjects. Humans of course presuppose many universal-general attributes of their fellows but no field of inquiry by scientific and academic specialists is necessary to discover these. When sociologists strive to enumerate them in propositional forms emulating natural science, historians and humanists frequently accuse them of banality. Such critics have been less prone to do so since Fernand Braudel and his *Annales* school of "social historians" have explored the past embodiments of precisely the kinds of phenomena sociologists investigate in the present.

The causes of particular wars, revolutions, elections and other timebound events are illuminated by universal-general propositions stating the necessary conditions for their occurrence. But the highly particular sufficient conditions accounting for their actual happening arouse our most intense interest. In the crucial twentieth century example of Hitler's coming to power, the unique ensemble of sufficient conditions continues to attract the greatest interest as opposed to the general preconditions for the rise of powerful dictators. Sociologists, especially the early social evolutionists, have often identified sequences of social change, or "stage" theories, as law-like equivalents of the propositions of natural science. Later critics have dubbed this "temperocentrism" as a version of overall Western ethnocentrism, but the prevalent labels of "developing" and underdeveloped" echo such theories in taking the West as their societal counter model.

Marxism is obviously the most complex and influential stage theory, which only lost its full credibility with the collapse of the Soviet Union and its national satellites in 1989-1991. Socialists who had been the earliest critics of the Soviet model as debasing "true socialism" as well as even surviving "socialist" states based on that model (such as China, North Korea, and Cuba) ceased to regard "capitalism" as a homogeneous "system" that had to be abolished in its entirety and introduced capitalist elements into their own economies. The frequent conflation of capitalism with the less invidious term "market economy" is, however, not defensible, for partially "free" markets, that is, the exchange by private producers of good and services with money as the means of exchange, have existed in all societies above the primitive tribal level. Capitalism as a form of market economy involves a minority of "private" owners of the means of production paying wages to laboring nonowners who produce goods or services that are then sold for a profit that accrues only to the owners. Sociology came into being to explain the effects of the "great transformation" (Polanyi), but, in contrast to the earlier social evolutionists —Comte Spencer, and more ambiguously Marx—the first sociologists, emerging at a later date, were less inclined to celebrate "the great transformation" as progress. They were disposed to stress its underside, the negative effects of the decline of "community," anomie, and the emergence of new class hierarchies. More recent sociologists have used the broader more abstract terms "modernization" and "globalization" which are now the most general labels applied to the world's societies. Even the more precisely measured theory of the " demographic transition" over-generalized the experience of the West while correctly recognizing that mortality levels are more susceptible to reduction than fertility. However, the timing and duration of demographic change was vastly accelerated by new medical techniques, the spread of better contraceptive methods, and advances in agriculture, communications, and transportation.

The category of "subhistorical" might refer with no invidious intent to generalizations about particular existing societies for which there obviously can be no certain knowledge of how long they are likely to survive or to spread to new areas. This category covers the bulk of sociological research. Obviously, sociologists do not necessarily assume that their research will lead to universal rather than to historically particular generalizations. It is erroneous therefore to conflate transhistorical and subhistorical generalizations because both refer to open classes and then to group sociology with the sciences and history with the humanities. Sociologists by using methods of direct observation obviously unavailiable to historians have nevertheless greatly broadened and added depth to the content of historical scholarship. Historians, most notably the so-called "social historians," have been moved to seek out data comparable to that of the sociologists though clearly more limited and less reliable.

One might say that the sociologist searches for the *necessary* conditions for the existence of durable social phenomena while the historian seeks the inevitably historically specific *sufficient* conditions. The explanation of *any* social phenomenon thus synthesizes the general and the particular rather than subsuming the latter under the former. We usually are most keenly anxious to identify the latter exemplifying Martha Nussbaum's "priority of the particular." That has been the major theme of this book while granting that historical explanations are improved and achieve greater depth by their sensitivity to broad generalizations.

Index